SOUTH DOWNS
WAY

SOUTH DOWNS WAY

Paul Millmore

Photographs by Martin Page
General editor Michael Allaby

AURUM PRESS

COUNTRYSIDE COMMISSION · ORDNANCE SURVEY

ACKNOWLEDGEMENTS

My thanks go to all the staff of the three county councils along the Way, but particularly to Phil Belden, Alan Stevens, Nigel Kitchener, Andrew Woodcock, David Marshall, Paul Smith, Tony Appicella and Bill Bide. Also to the regional tourist boards, the Society of Sussex Downsmen, John Dakin, Peter Brandon, John Boardman, the Nature Conservancy Council, Walter and Vivien Long, Alison Bullar, Mary Parker, Glyn Jones and Chris Fairbrother. Special thanks go to Linda Bacon, Debby Emery and Romy Luffman, who all helped with the typing, and to the extremely patient editor, Michael Allaby. Thanks also to my daughter Tamsin and my wife Bridget for keeping me company along parts of the route and for putting up with me during the writing of this book!

This book is dedicated to Gideon and Rowan Millmore who journeyed with me in spirit.

Paul Millmore is Countryside Management Officer for East Sussex County Council. For the last 15 years he has been involved with the conservation of the South Downs in East Sussex. He is currently campaigning for the whole area to be made a national park.

This edition first published 1990 by Aurum Press Ltd in association with the Countryside Commission and the Ordnance Survey
Text copyright © 1990 by Aurum Press Ltd, the Countryside Commission and the Ordnance Survey
Maps Crown copyright © 1990 by the Ordnance Survey
Photographs copyright © 1990 by the Countryside Commission

British Library Cataloguing in Publication Data
Millmore, Paul
South Downs Way – (National trail guides; 12)
1. East & West Sussex. Long-distance footpaths & long-distance bridleways: South Downs Way. Visitors' guides
I. Title   II. Allaby, Michael 1933–   III. Series
914.22'6

ISBN 1 85410 099 8
OS ISBN 0 319 00194 6

Book design by Robert Updegraff
Cover photograph: 'Jack & Jill' windmills at Clayton, West Sussex
Title page photograph: the footpath section of the Way goes along the cliff edge of the Seven Sisters

Typeset by Wyvern Typesetting Ltd, Bristol
Printed and bound in Italy by Printers Srl, Trento

CONTENTS

Circular walks appear on pages 46, 68 and 120

How to use this guide

This guide to the 99-mile (160-kilometre) South Downs Way is in three parts:

- The introduction, with an historical background to the area and advice for walkers, horseriders and cyclists.

- The Way itself, split into eleven chapters, with maps opposite the description for each route section. The distances noted with each chapter represent the total length of the South Downs Way, including sections through towns and villages. This part of the guide also includes information on places of interest as well as a number of short walks which can be taken around parts of the path. Key sites are numbered both in the text and on the maps to make it easier to follow the route description.

- The last part includes useful information such as local transport, accommodation and organisations involved with the South Downs Way.

The maps have been prepared by the Ordnance Survey for this trail guide using 1:25000 Pathfinder or Outdoor Leisure maps as a base. The line of the South Downs Way is shown in yellow, with the status of each section of the trail – footpath or bridleway, for example – shown in green underneath (see key on inside front cover). These rights of way markings also indicate the precise alignment of the South Downs Way, which you should follow. In some cases, the yellow line on these maps may show a route that is different from that shown on older maps; you are recommended to follow the yellow route in this guide, which will be the route that is waymarked with the distinctive acorn symbol ♟ used for all national trails. Any parts of the South Downs Way that may be difficult to follow on the ground are clearly highlighted in the route description, and important points to watch for are marked with letters in each chapter, both in the text and on the maps. *Some maps start on a right-hand page and continue on the left-hand page – black arrows (➤) at the edge of the maps indicate the start point.*

Should there be a need to divert the South Downs Way from the route shown in this guide, for maintenance work or because the route has had to be changed, you are advised to follow any waymarks or signs along the path.

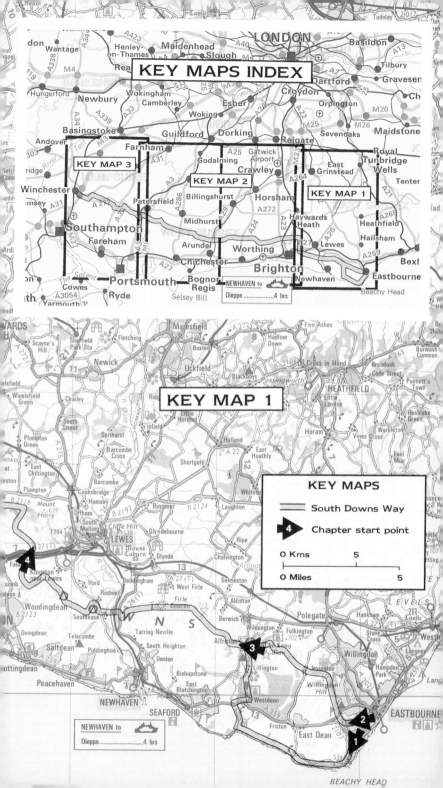

KEY MAP 3

Distance checklist

This list will assist you in calculating the distances between your proposed overnight accommodation and in checking your progress along the walk.

location	approx. distance from previous location	
footpath section	miles	km
Eastbourne	0	0
Birling Gap	3.8	6.1
Exceat	3.9	6.3
Westdean	0.4	0.6
Litlington	1.6	2.6
Alfriston	1.1	1.8
bridleway section		
Eastbourne	0	0
Jevington	3.6	5.8
Alfriston	3.8	6.1
Southease railway station	7.0	11.3
Southease	0.6	1.0
Telscombe Youth Hostel (off route)	1.7	2.7
Rodmell	0.6	1.0
Newmarket Inn	5.3	8.5
Lewes railway station (off route)	2.5	4.0
Ditchling Beacon	5.3	8.5
Ditchling (off route)	1.3	2.1
Clayton Windmills	1.8	2.9
Pyecombe	1.4	2.3
Devil's Dyke	2.5	4.0
Tottington Barn Youth Hostel	2.6	4.2
A283 (water point) for Upper Beeding	1.6	2.6
Upper Beeding (off route)	0.8	1.3
Steyning (off route)	2.0	3.2
Chanctonbury Ring	5.3	8.5
A24 bus stop/car park	1.5	2.4
Washington	0.6	1.0
Chantry Post car park	2.2	3.5
via Washington	3.1	5.0
Warningcamp Youth Hostel (off route)	5.0	8.0

Amberley railway station	4.1	6.6
Warningcamp Youth Hostel (off route) (via North Stoke and river bank)	4.0	6.4
Arundel (off route) (via river bank)	4.6	7.4
Toby's Stone (Bignor Hill)	3.6	5.8
Bignor Hill car park (Stane Street)	0.6	1.0
Littleton Farm (A285)	2.1	3.4
Tegleaze Post	0.9	1.4
Graffham Post	1.1	1.8
Cocking Hill car park	3.3	5.3
Wealdan Downland Museum (off route)	2.8	4.5
Cocking (off route)	0.7	1.1
Devil's Jumps Ancient Monument	3.2	5.1
Hookway (public house) (off route)	0.7	1.1
Harting Hill car park	4.0	6.4
South Harting (off route)	0.7	1.1
county boundary (Hampshire/West Sussex)	2.0	3.2
Queen Elizabeth Country Park	1.9	3.1
Buriton Church (off route)	0.5	0.8
Ancient Farm Project	2.0	3.2
Butser Hill	0.8	1.3
HMS *Mercury*	2.5	4.0
Old Winchester Hill (Nature Reserve)	4.2	6.8
Exton	2.7	4.3
Milbury's (public house)	4.1	6.6
Cheesefoot Head car park	4.6	7.4
Winchester Youth Hostel	3.4	5.5

Preface

The South Downs Way is one of the national trails in England and Wales that the Countryside Commission promotes for walkers or riders to explore and enjoy the best of our countryside, far away from towns, traffic and the bustle of urban life.

These trails are particularly suited for long journeys, but they can also be sampled on an afternoon or over a weekend. Another way of using them is as part of a round trip, or circular walk, and suggestions for these are included in this guide. National trails are maintained by local authorities on behalf of the Commission, and are well waymarked with our distinctive acorn. Each trail provides an enjoyable, and sometimes challenging, walk or ride in the countryside.

National trails run through the grandest and most beautiful countryside and coast which England and Wales have to offer. Many of them also link with other waymarked paths, thus making it possible to plan a variety of journeys throughout the countryside.

We hope you will enjoy walking or riding along the South Downs Way and that this guide will help to make your journey one to remember.

Sir Derek Barber
Chairman
Countryside Commission

At Cocking Down the route is a broad trackway through arable fields.

PART ONE

INTRODUCTION

Pleasures along the South Downs Way

In the late 20th century why would anyone want to walk or ride 99 miles (160 km) along the South Downs Way between Eastbourne and Winchester?

There may be far easier methods of travel available but, to journey along this ancient route, away from the traffic, noise and dirt of the main roads, is an experience not to be missed. The pressures of modern urban life seem to put stresses on the human mind while failing adequately to exercise the body. To step back in time, and voyage by simple means along this historic ridgetop, is one of the best ways of reviving the spirit.

The sheer sense of space on top of the Downs is hard to describe. On clear days you can see so far, and from such a height, that it is almost like flying. In early morning or evening light, strong shadows give the rounded outlines of these hills a special texture. Whatever the time of year there are so many sights to discover: Saxon and Norman churches, tumuli (the graves of settlers from over 3,000 years ago), medieval field systems where meagre crops were grown, and dew ponds from the days of the huge 18th and 19th century sheep flocks.

Seeing sheep still grazing the Downs and the butterflies feeding on the wild flowers gives the traveller a tremendous sense of continuity. High on top of the dry, streamless hills you can get closer to the mind of the shepherd, pedlar or pilgrim who journeyed on this path centuries ago.

The South Downs Way is a particularly attractive national trail for the uninitiated. You can quickly achieve a feeling of quiet isolation, even solitude, while actually staying close to civilisation. The path is well used in summer, but as soon as you turn off the Way, into the heart of the Downs, there are opportunities to discover your own special places.

The underlying chalk geology makes this path one of the best for all-year-round journeys in Britain. The ground may be a little sticky in winter, but generally it is not a quagmire! It is easy to see why the Downs were chosen as ancient highways.

For the day or weekend traveller, the South Downs are ideally suited because of their accessibility. You can put a mountain bike on the train in London and, in just over an hour, get off at Glynde, Berwick or Lewes stations, all on the edge of these magnificent hills.

The other main attraction of the South Downs – to the uninitiated or unfit – is that, overall, the walking, riding and cycling are easy! All the paths are generally well-maintained. They are not overgrown and the stiles and gates are in good repair and clearly waymarked. In fact, the Downs have such a good path network that it is not difficult to take quite small children along with you. This is the ideal family area for exploring the countryside – at the eastern end you even have the sea!

West Sussex County Council organises group walks over the whole length of the route and if you join the Society of Sussex Downsmen you can participate in their annual Easter walk (see pages 165 and 167 for addresses).

Downland wildlife

The combination of shallow, dry, chalk soils and low nutrient levels, due to constant grazing by sheep, has created a man-made habitat – effectively a grass desert. This 'desert' can now be seen only in remnants along the scarp slopes and sections of the Downs too steep for arable farming.

Surprisingly, this inhospitable habitat supports a huge variety of plants especially adapted to the environment. Where no fertilisers have been applied, up to 50 species can be found in each square yard. Sit on undisturbed chalk grassland in the summer and, among the sheep's fescue and upright brome grass, you will find flowering plants with strange names such as salad burnet, squinancywort, round-headed rampion, scabious, and autumn lady's tresses. In spring you can still find thousands of cowslips, while later in the summer, attracted by food plants, over 20 species of butterfly, including silver-spotted skippers and adonis blues, can be seen. Insects other than butterflies are also common and close inspection of chalk grassland will reveal many types of snails, moths and grass-hoppers. Useful indicators of undisturbed, herb-rich grassland are the hills of the yellow meadow ant. These low grassy lumps, about one foot (30 cm) high, show that the ground has not been ploughed for many years.

When farmers forget to spray, even arable fields can be beautiful.

The observant traveller can find early purple and common spotted orchids, and with more care you might see burnt, fragrant, pyramidal, frog, musk, bee and green-winged varieties.

Almost certainly you will see rooks nesting in the ash and beech woodland or feeding on the corn stubble, jackdaws and seagulls at Beachy Head, skylarks everywhere, and kestrels hovering above looking for a juicy beetle. Pheasant and partridge are often disturbed, and in the valleys there are herons fishing in the drainage ditches and cormorants on the rivers.

Fortunately, much of the Downs has recently been declared an Environmentally Sensitive Area and farmers are encouraged by grant aid to move back to traditional grazing with no fertilisers or pesticides.

Geology

Most people think of the Downs as a smooth, almost treeless, landscape. The rocks that form the Downs and Weald are made from sediments, laid down in both freshwater lakes and seas many millions of years ago, then raised by earth movements and bent into a huge dome about 125 miles (200 km) long and 50 miles (80 km) wide. Being soft, it began to be eroded by the rain and wind as soon as it was raised above the sea. This natural erosion is still going on today.

The top layer of the sedimentary sandwich was chalk, with some younger deposits, made up of the remains of shells of creatures that lived in the warm Cretaceous seas, during a period so long that sediments hundreds of yards thick were deposited. Their scale can best be seen where the modern sea has sliced through the chalk along the cliffs between Beachy Head and Cuckmere Haven. After winter storms have caused cliff falls it is possible to find among the rocks fossilised shells of animals that lived 75 million years ago. The chalk is not only being eroded where the sea meets it today, but also where the top is exposed to the elements. Over time the dome has worn away, and all that remains of the chalk deposits are the North and South Downs.

How did the rivers cut through the Downs? Why are there valleys without streams or rivers in them? Where do all the flints come from?

The great dome was formed very slowly and the Cuckmere, Ouse, Adur and Arun Rivers had time to cut their way through the soft chalk. The valleys without streams, such as Devil's Dyke, were clearly cut by water, either in a much wetter climate, which would have led to a higher water table, or during the Ice Ages, when permafrost would have made the chalk temporarily impervious.

Today the chalk is filled with rainwater like a huge sponge, and towns such as Eastbourne and Brighton derive most of their drinking water from these underground sources. However, in the wetter parts of the year, streams do flow in some of the dry valleys, and the 'Winterbourne', which rises near the New-market Inn and flows through Lewes to the River Ouse, is a classic example.

Flint, which is the only hard and brittle rock to be found on the Downs, is a remarkable material – basically silica that was precipitated by chemical processes and replaced the chalk (calcium carbonate) around it. As the chalk eroded, the lumps of hard flint were left behind. It was probably once liquid, as it forms in organic shapes and has been known to fill the voids left by dead sea creatures to form 'flint' fossils. When you visit the cliffs it is possible to see clear seams of flints laid down as narrow bands in the chalk. Shortly after ploughing some of the fields of the Downs have the appearance of a stony wasteland, as flints rise to the surface.

Flints may seem simply to be a hard surfacing to the down-land trackways, but their importance in terms of human development should not be underestimated. Early people found that they could use the razor-sharp edges of flaked flint as a cutting tool and over many thousands of years they refined their techniques until quite sophisticated knives, arrowheads and axes could be made. Such was the importance of this mineral that it led to the establishment of specialised industrial workings, such as the flint mines on Windover Hill, and the early development of trade over a wide area. It was perhaps the presence of flint on the Downs that led to this area being the focus of early British civilisation. The later use of flint with iron to 'strike a light', and thus make fire-lighting relatively simple, combined with the use of the sparks from flint and iron in early flint-lock guns, confirmed the position of this odd, little under-stood mineral as one of the great keys to European de-velopment.

With no hard rock present on the Downs, flint has also been the only naturally occurring building material, and in its various forms is very much part of the rural landscape.

The wave-cut platform beneath the Seven Sisters cliffs is part of a Voluntary Marine Conservation Area.

History of the Downs

Between 500,000 and 12,000 years ago (the Old Stone Age), small numbers of nomadic people occasionally wandered the Downs and coastal fringe, hunting deer, wild boar, birds and fish. It was pretty bleak then and the climate shifted back and forth between long periods of freezing cold, during the Ice Ages, and temperate conditions. The ice never spread south far enough to cover the Downs, but its influence made the vegetation tundra-like. When the ice finally melted 10,000 years ago, forests developed and the still-nomadic population of the Middle Stone Age grew.

The land bridge that had linked Britain to the Continent was finally breached by the rising sea.

Then, roughly 5,000 years ago, the New Stone Age (Neolithic) people crossed the narrow sea and settled the Downs. They brought with them a new, more sophisticated culture, which included semi-nomadic agriculture, pottery, flint mining and trade. This fundamental shift from simple hunters and gatherers to a tribal people who kept domestic animals and cleared the trees to grow crops began changing the Downs from forested hills to the open rolling landscape we see today.

You will pass many landscape features that date from Neolithic times (around 3000 BC). There are large enclosures at Combe Hill (above Jevington) and Barkhale (on Bignor Hill). Archaeological excavations suggest that these were put to a variety of uses, including settlements, meeting places, stock-gathering grounds and ceremonial events. Another remarkable group of Neolithic features occasionally to be found along the Way are long barrows. These earth mounds, up to 200 feet (60 metres) long and sited on dominant hills, were the communal graves of extended families or clan groups.

Around 2500 BC, communal graves gave way to single burials in the form of round barrows, marked on the maps as 'tumuli'. There are many hundreds of these low, circular mounds on the high ground along the South Downs Way. Between 2000 BC, when the first tumuli were constructed, and 1000 BC a more advanced Bronze Age civilisation developed, based on settled agriculture with farmsteads of round buildings surrounded by a rectangular field. Such a settlement of 13 round huts within a protective fence was established on Itford Hill around 1000 BC and there was a similar settlement at Plumpton Plain.

This high, dry route along the top of the Downs must have been an important part of the Bronze Age trading network that brought jet from Yorkshire, gold from Ireland and amber from Scandinavia. Over a dozen hoards of bronze tools and weapons have been found on the Sussex Downs and they confirm the Way as a significant trade route.

The Bronze Age economy was based on mixed farming and there are many landscape features of this period along the route. The 'cross dykes' were probably farm boundaries, and the large enclosures that are visible may have been stock pens of some kind, such as those at Butser Hill and Belle Tout.

Around 650 BC iron began to be used, and as Celtic settlers from the Continent brought more of the new metal with them, a further cultural and technological change took place. Nevertheless, the Iron Age people lived very similar lives to those of the Bronze Age, with round houses and settled agriculture, but the population grew and some sort of crop rotation and fertilisation of the arable land evolved. More than 60 Iron Age farmsteads are known in Sussex and the increasing population, equipped with sharp, iron tools, probably led to more of the remaining chalk woodland being cleared for agriculture or felled for fuel.

The most obvious Iron Age monuments are the camps and hill forts built around 300–200 BC. It is now believed that these forts were the product of tribal rivalry. They are all on high, defensive positions and consisted of a circular bank and ditches. Some are relatively small and simple, like that at Chanctonbury, but there are more elaborate forts at Devil's Dyke, Old Winchester Hill and Cissbury Ring.

The field systems created by the Iron Age farmers were a common downland sight until modern methods led to their being ploughed out. The best remaining examples to be seen from the Way are on the flanks of Combe Hill, near Jevington, and at Balmer Down, near Brighton. These small rectangular fields (usually less than 2 acres or 1 hectare) are still noticeable, because they were farmed for so long that they effectively formed blocks of terraces with clear lynchets (banks) up to 10 feet (3 metres) high.

Sussex and the downland area were also very important to the Romans. This area was a strategic bridgehead for the conquest of the rest of Britain and it was commercially vital for iron from the Weald and corn and meat from the Downs. There are still remains of Roman roads running from Chichester and Lewes to London; Roman villas, such as that at Bignor, and country houses and farmsteads have been found all along the scarp foot.

Generally, little changed for the local downland people, but during this settled period they started to establish significant hamlets and villages for the first time.

Sussex was one of the first parts of Roman Britain to be conquered and colonised by the Saxons. *The Anglo-Saxon Chronicle* tells us that a small band of Saxons came by ship and landed somewhere between Beachy Head and Selsey Bill around 477. But instead of developing the high Downs, which had already been farmed for over 2,000 years, they opted for the better soils of the downland valleys and scarp foot.

Each long, narrow parish had land for pigs and cattle in the clay Weald – arable land at the scarp foot and sheep grazing on the Downs. Walking along the South Downs Way you can see at a glance whole parishes that formed the basis of the early Anglo-Saxon settlement of southern Sussex.

Tracks, or 'droveways', developed between the villages at the foot of the Downs and the Wealden pastures. If you look at the Ordnance Survey maps these parallel, north–south roads are quite clear and some pass distinctly through gaps in the Downs or tracks cut across the scarp, as at Chanctonbury, Storrington, Steyning and Rackham Bank.

Between the 8th and 9th centuries there was a reorganisation of this scattered peasant population into nucleated villages, so that they could communally farm the land more effectively. Large areas of lighter soils around the village sites would have been cleared, and these islands of cultivation within woodland at the scarp foot would have been visible from the South Downs Way. However, the High Weald would still have been largely forest, even at the time of the Norman Conquest in 1066.

The Sussex Saxons rejected Christianity for longer than people in other parts of England, but once they had accepted it they quickly built churches, unpretentious structures made of local materials. The Normans continued this Christian tradition and by 1086 a parish church was an integral part of every Sussex village.

From the Norman invasion until the Black Death of 1348 was a period of population expansion. The existing communities grew and new market towns and seaports were established. The Church owned huge estates and the large barns at Alciston, Wilmington and Bishopstone attest to its efficient farming methods. It was in this period that the basic system of downland

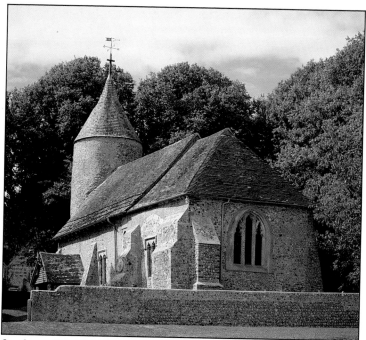

Southease Church has an unusual circular Saxon tower.

sheep combined with scarp-foot corn was developed. Each day the shepherd brought his flock off the hill tops and penned them on the stubble and fallow of the arable soil at the base of the Downs. This system of using sheep as a 'mobile dunging machine' created a profitable and sustainable farming system. The wool was worked into cloth by artisans in the Weald or traded across the Channel with Flanders.

The plague of the 14th century severely reduced the population. Some villages, such as Exceat, became completely deserted and many others, such as Botolphs and Coombes, shrank in size. The downland continued to be farmed but the large peasant population it once supported declined, and by the end of the 17th century one single sheep 'ranch' commonly occupied a whole parish.

Another influence on the downland landscape was the 17th and 18th century growth of chalk quarrying, to lime the acid Wealden land and to provide building mortar. This was combined with a brief period of canal building and improved river navigation on the Arun and Ouse, to move the chalk from the downland quarries to the Weald.

Many isolated flint 'manure' barns were built between 1780 and 1840 to house the oxen used for ploughing and to hold the increased corn harvest of this period.

The growth of the resorts from little more than fishing towns was due to turnpike road improvements and to sea-bathing becoming fashionable. Surprisingly, in the 18th century the open nature of the downland landscape was no longer popular and considerable sums were spent on landscaping, as at Stanmer Park. The resorts were given huge impetus by the Napoleonic Wars – not only was it impossible to visit the Continent, but also troops were stationed along the coast, providing a richer social life in the seaside towns. This, combined with royal patronage and the coming of the railway, led to much of the coastal fringe of the Downs being covered in housing. Places such as Brighton, Hove and Worthing outstripped the county towns in size. Fortunately, this process, combined with the lack of 19th century industrial development, stopped the growth of the older towns and has left us with such gems as Lewes, Chichester and Arundel.

By the end of the 19th century, cheap food from Australia and the prairies of North America had made downland farming unprofitable. Much of the arable land reverted to sheep grazing or scrub and some farmers began to sell off their land to property developers.

Between 1900 and 1945 residential development spread on to some of the remaining parts of the downland coastline. Eventually the despoliation was so great that individuals, charities, and local authorities bought the land between Eastbourne and Seaford in order to protect it. The Town and Country Planning Act 1947 brought speculative house building under control. Since then, the route you follow between Beachy Head and Winchester has been further protected in various ways. The Downs have been designated an area of outstanding natural beauty and there are a number of national and local nature reserves. Much of the scarp is a site of special scientific interest. Many of the buildings have been listed and the best remaining undamaged archaeological features are scheduled ancient monuments.

Despite all these conservation measures, the destruction of the old downland by 'high tech' agriculture has happened on a scale, and at a speed, never before contemplated. Nevertheless, today's traveller will find these rolling hills, with their mixture of corn, woods and grassland, immensely beautiful.

Practical advice

The most important basic rule to follow is 'keep it light'. The temptation to take too much equipment on a long journey, or even a day trip, should be strongly resisted. In winter the winds can be biting, so a warm, waterproof hat or hood is essential – ideally it should shelter the ears! Some form of lightweight, windproof, wet-weather gear is also necessary, preferably something that breathes. It is also important to be warm; long underwear, wool trousers and jumpers help. If your top clothes have front zips or buttons they can be opened if you get too hot. In summer some form of comfortable shade is vital. Remember to have long shirt sleeves, so that they can be rolled down to protect arms from sunburn.

Plan your route, especially if travelling for several days. Each section of this guide covers a comfortable day's walking in winter light. Cyclists and horseriders can obviously cover greater distances. Get all the extra maps you require if you intend to go off the edge of those in this guide. Youth hostels can be full all year round, so try to book in advance. Enquire locally about bed and breakfast accommodation. There are a number of camp sites along the Way (though none as yet in the Hampshire section). If asked, most farmers will give permission to camp.

A compass is very useful – it looks complicated but at least it will tell you where north is. If you get completely lost in thick mist or fog on the Way (which is unlikely), walk any path northward and you are sure to hit a road.

Carry some liquid refreshment – a flask of hot tea in winter or some water in summer – and a snack. Water points are marked in the guide but the distance between them can be considerable. Your basic minimal equipment should include: this guide book; a compass to help you follow the directions in this guide; a small first-aid kit (plasters for blisters and crêpe bandage for strains); a whistle, just in case you need to give the recognised distress signal of 6 blasts – 3 in reply; a small torch with new batteries – there is nothing worse than flat batteries if you are stuck at night; a small day pack or saddle bags for carrying all this equipment (try to keep it below 22 lbs/10 kgs); lightweight wet-weather clothing – especially in the winter; boots or strong shoes you know are comfortable (do not try to break in a pair of new boots by walking the whole South Downs Way – you are guaranteed to get blisters!); a pair of dry socks; a watch,

Looking down into the valley of the Arun.

31

to ensure correct bus and train connections; refreshments; emergency loo paper; a hat.

You may also wish to take: a map case for wet weather; suntan lotion in summer; gloves; field guides; binoculars (lightweight); camera and film; tent and sleeping bag (as lightweight as possible) if camping; sunglasses – the glare from bare chalk or snow can be quite strong; penknife.

It is sensible to eat a substantial breakfast before setting out, as you cannot be sure of arriving at a pub or café exactly at lunch time. Nowadays most pubs serve food and one of the joys of a day's journey on the Downs is to drop down off the top to a scarp-foot or valley-floor village and eat a good meal before setting off for the afternoon. Some pubs also have family rooms, offer camping for walkers on the Way, and sometimes serve evening meals.

The larger towns all have excellent facilities. Eastbourne, Brighton and Winchester are within easy reach of the Downs and offer a variety of shopping, as well as specialist shops for cyclists and riders. The county town of Lewes lies close to the South Downs Way. It, and also Arundel, has quite a reasonable range of shops, and hotels and bed and breakfast accommodation. Many smaller villages have a general store and post office combined.

Wednesday is often half-day closing. In the larger towns many shops stay open but in the smaller centres most are closed in the afternoon.

Cyclists

Obviously a good quality, all-terrain bike with 18 or 21 gears is best, but in summer it is possible to cycle along the Way on an ordinary bike with tough tyres. This does involve a lot of pushing up hills, and really 12 gears is the minimum requirement.

The cyclist needs to take certain basic extra equipment – the following is advised: a lightweight safety helmet (if you come off and hit your head on a flint, it could be rather nasty!); a good basic tool kit, including puncture repair, spare brake pads, at least one spare inner tube and oil for lubricating the chain; a handlebar map holder can save a lot of fiddling about, as can waterbottles fixed to the bike; panniers well secured to the bike rather than a day sack.

Choose the right clothing for the trip. In summer, wear something that is easy to open or put on and take off. Shorts are more comfortable than long trousers in summer, but not necessarily on the tougher narrow sections, where nettles can be a problem.

Hiking boots are heavy and trainers offer no ankle support on the flinty surfaces when pushing a bike uphill. Special mountain-biking boots are best, but some sort of lightweight rambling boot would be a reasonable compromise. As with walking, keep gear to a minimum.

A few helpful tips: if you have your tyres pumped up too hard, the ride is uncomfortable but, if they are too soft, the flints cut the side walls; if you get a puncture from a thorn and do not realise that this has happened, when you put the repaired tube back in the tyre it will immediately puncture again; if cycling during the winter, watch out for your tyre pump getting clogged up with mud. See page 157 for shops specialising in spare parts for bikes.

Horseriders

Wear footwear that you know is comfortable. Rubber boots tend to make your feet sweat and are cold in winter. A long, wet-weather riding coat or cape with hood is needed for bad weather and a hard hat that fits well is essential. A peak on your hat will offer some additional shade in summer.

Good, new shoes on a fit horse are, of course, basic, and all your tack should be in tip-top condition. Road studs (not the screw-in type, to avoid jarring the horse) might be helpful in icy conditions. Carry some feed (nuts are less bulky than oats). And a particularly useful item is a rope halter or head halter to tie up your horse while you have your own meals.

There is a good deal of thorn and blackthorn along sections of the Way, so strong riding trousers are needed and leather chapps can protect your legs even more. Shoes are better than boots if you have to walk any distance, and if you wear short boots or riding shoes, leather gaiters will help.

Saddles for long-distance riding have a wider seat than standard; some people prefer western-style kit for comfort. It is possible to get sheepskin covers that slip over your saddle and can significantly reduce long-distance soreness. Rubbing reins can be abrasive, so gloves are useful, not only for warmth but also for offering some protection.

Saddle bags are the best way to carry your gear and some saddle cloths have pockets that are ideal for your guide and other items.

A small grooming kit, of a dandy brush and hoof pick, and a first-aid kit for horses is essential. Your horse may be cut by flints above the fetlocks while crossing ploughed fields, so take antibiotic powder in a puffer and bandages.

You can ride the Eastbourne to Buriton section of the Way in a weekend on a fit horse. The extension to Winchester will add a day, once it is open to riders. Naturally, the journey can be taken at a more leisurely pace and sometimes stony ground makes walking necessary.

Get off once an hour for about five minutes to rest both yourself and the horse. When you stop, loosen the girth and resettle the saddle. This lets the blood in the horse's back recirculate. After long-distance riding it is vital to take proper care of your horse. To avoid serious swelling do not remove the saddle straight away: leave it for five to ten minutes to allow the blood to return slowly, rather than in a rush. After removing, slap the back where the saddle was, to help blood circulation.

To help your horse relax and dry off at the end of the day, finish your journey at a walk. Let the girth out a single hole shortly before you stop. Initially it is important to let your horse drink no more than half a bucket of water, in order to avoid colic. If your horse is tired, keep it dry and warm, especially if you have had to sponge it down. At night remember to visit your horse regularly to make sure it has not started to sweat.

The cathedral at Winchester, the Saxon capital of England, which lies at the western end of the national trail.

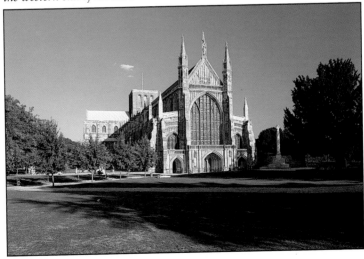

PART TWO

SOUTH DOWNS WAY

1 Eastbourne to Alfriston

Footpath section: *via Birling Gap and Litlington*
10¾ miles (17.2 km)

The South Downs Way footpath starts at the western end of Eastbourne promenade. If you decide to begin the walk here, remember that Beachy Head Youth Hostel is actually 2 miles (3.5 km) north of the Head itself.

It is possible to get buses to the start, but if you want to walk, follow the signpost from the station to Beachy Head up Grove Road, past the Town Hall and through the Meads district. Alternatively, go south-east to the sea front, so you can see the pier and Martello tower as you head westwards along the promenade.

The Way begins next to a small kiosk **A**, shuttered in winter, but where in summer you can buy refreshments. It takes about half an hour of gentle walking from the railway station to reach this point.

The path rises steeply as a thin chalky line, through downland and scattered scrub. To the south lies the Channel stretching out to the horizon. On a clear day, looking east, you can see as far as Hastings, the Fairlight Cliffs, perhaps even Dungeness. The windswept thorns show what a bleak spot this can be.

About 220 yards (200 metres) from the kiosk, after climbing a flight of concrete steps, you come to a waymark post. Carry on another 30 yards to a junction of paths. Take the southernmost of two forks and head into the scrub towards another waymark post. As you rise, the wind can pick up. The scrub, with its stunted thorn, ash and sycamore, offers some shelter, but in summer this can be a hot, steep climb, though there are wild raspberries to help you along!

Go south-westwards, with fire rides creating a maze of paths. The ground falls steeply away to the south into Whitebread Hole, a scrub-filled combe. This is a safe haven for birds migrating across the Channel. In winter there are fine tufts of old man's beard strung among the branches and magpies flit among the trees. There is an abundance of purple rosebay willowherb which, in season, sends great drifts of white seed blowing across the Downs.

As you reach the edge of the scrub you can see cars driving along the Beachy Head road. Here you pass another waymark post and walk a short distance on open grassland in a south-

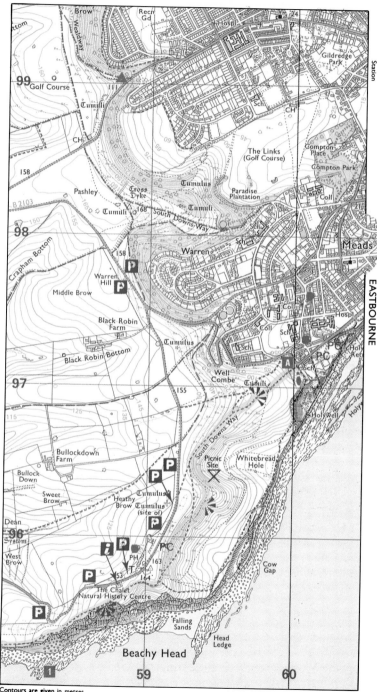

Contours are given in metres
The vertical interval is 5m

37

Belle Tout ceased functioning as a lighthouse in 1901 and is now a private house.

easterly direction. Down below lie the playing fields on the floor of Whitebread Hole. About 55 yards (50 metres) ahead, a waymark directs you into the scrub again along a narrow, sloping path that follows the contours. Occasionally the thorn thins out and the views down to the sea are superb. On the skyline above is the coastguard radio mast. There is lots of poisonous climbing white bryony and, in the more open areas, chalk downland flowers. After 550 yards (500 metres) you come to a stretch of crumbling tarmac and cross the lighter-coloured 'peace' path twice (commemorating United Nations Peace Year). From here, the trail dips round the head of a cut-off dry valley. To the north is the main car park with nearby public toilet and Beachy Head Inn. In the summer refreshments are also available at the adjoining café.

At Beachy Head you occasionally see hang gliders. To the west you can make out Belle Tout, which was the lighthouse for this stretch of coast between 1834 and 1901. A small bungalow presently houses a visitor centre. The octagonal brick shelter nearby was a 19th century signalling station. From here messages were sent to the London offices of Lloyd's brokers confirming the safe arrival of ships and cargoes.

As you pass, walk south-westwards towards the cliff edge. If you don't suffer from vertigo, look down 530 feet (160 metres) to the 'candy stick' Beachy Head lighthouse **1**. In misty weather the noise of the foghorn gives the whole area an eerie atmosphere. The lighthouse was built in 1902 by steam-winching huge stone blocks from the top of the cliffs down to the sea. (In the Lighthouse Bar of the Beachy Head Inn there is a series of photos showing how it was constructed.)

From this viewpoint the South Downs Way follows the cliff line westwards to Birling Gap. The sea can be stained a milky white by the eroding chalk and, when the tide is out, you can see the flat, wave-cut platform. This is the only undeveloped stretch of coast left in south-east England and has been defined as a heritage coast by the Countryside Commission.

To the north lies Hodcombe Farm, a private house surrounded by stunted trees, and a favourite bird-ringing station for ornithologists. At Shooters' Bottom there are three yellow concrete markers in the turf. These indicators were used to measure rates of cliff erosion from aerial photographs.

Belle Tout **2** is now a private residence, but as part of the filming for a television series its canopy was replaced, so it still retains a maritime character. Eventually this redundant lighthouse will fall into the sea, but at the moment it remains a precarious landmark, with the Way passing on its landward side.

From here you get tremendous views of the Seven Sisters cliffs. To the west is a small building – the coastguard lookout – and you should head for that.

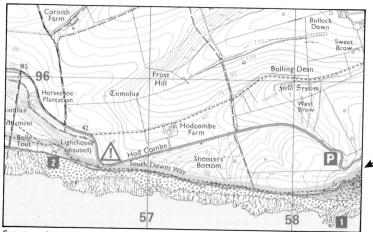

Contours are given in metres
The vertical interval is 5m

Next to the coastguard station is an information board giving brief details of the area known as Lookout Hill. When Bronze Age people lived in this region the cliffs would have been at least 1¼ miles (2 km) further out to sea. Down to the west is Birling Gap with its facilities of café, hotel, toilets, telephone and water point.

The Way turns north about 55 yards (50 metres) past the lookout and heads downhill to the main road. Turn south for 100 yards along the verge to reach Birling Gap itself. The National Trust acquired the Gap under its Enterprise Neptune scheme (set up to protect as much as possible of the most beautiful stretches of coastline in England and Wales) and has erected a viewing platform to help you see the Seven Sisters cliffs safely. There are also steps from this platform down to the beach.

From Birling Gap, the Way heads west again up a flinty track, past the new toilets which look like a tarred, fisherman's cottage. At the top, turn north where there is a waymark post directing you for approximately 50 yards and then, at the next waymark, turn west again.

Ahead is a gate leading on to Crowlink, the largest of the National Trust properties in East Sussex. Here you start walking the 'ups and downs' of the Seven Sisters. In the distance you can spot the brown clayey cap on the cliffs at Seaford Head Nature Reserve.

Going up the western slope of Michel Dean you come to a concrete obelisk **3** commemorating the gift of this land to the National Trust by W.A. Robertson. He donated this land in memory of his two brothers, who were killed on the Somme during the First World War; a wonderful way to remember the brave dead.

At Flagstaff Brow there is another monument made from a sarsen stone. This sandstone boulder was stranded on top of the chalk 50 million years ago when the rocks above were eroded. On it is a plaque commemorating a further gift, which allowed the National Trust to purchase the Crowlink Valley. Below the cliff, at Flagstaff Bottom, there is a raised area of the wave-cut platform marked on the map as Flagstaff Point. When the tide is out you realise why so many ships foundered along this coastline.

Gap Bottom **4** was another low point favoured by smugglers. You can just see the square outline of some now-demolished coastguard cottages.

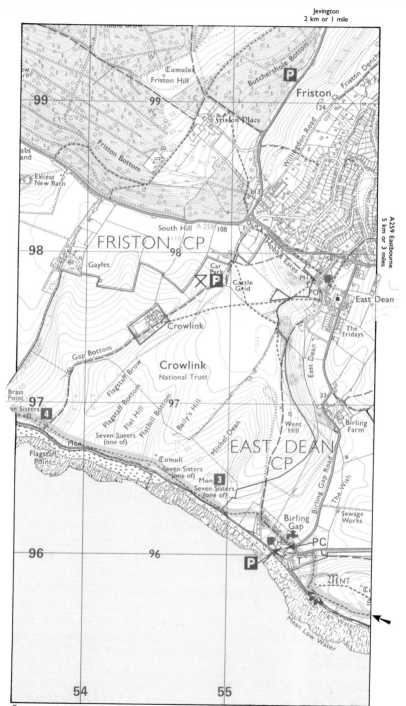

A259 Eastbourne
5 km or 3 miles

Butchershole Bottom

Friston

Tumulus
Friston Hill

99   99

W

Friston Place

Friston Dench

Willingdon Road

124

Exceat
New Barn

Friston Bottom

113

South Hill   A 259   108

FRISTON CP   98

98

Gayles

Hobbs Eares   PH

58

Car
Park   P

Cattle
Grid

PO

East Dean

The
Fridays

Crowlink

Gap Bottom

Crowlink

National Trust

East Dean

Flagstaff Brow

Brass
Point

en Sisters
(one of)   97   97   33

4

Flagstaff Bottom

Flat Hill

Flathill Bottom

Bally's Hill

Went
Hill

Birling
Farm

Flagstaff
Point

Mon

Seven Sisters
(one of)

75

Michel Dean

EAST DEAN
CP

Birling Gap Road

The Wish

Tumuli
Seven Sisters
(one of)

50

Mon   3

Seven Sisters
(one of)

Birling
Gap

Sewage
Works

96   96

Hotel

PC

P   T

NT

Mean High Water

Mean Low Water

54   55

Contours are given in metres
The vertical interval is 5m

41

The fence on the skyline at Brass Point marks the eastern boundary of Seven Sisters Country Park. Looking west from Rough Brow you can see the groynes of Cuckmere Haven and the cottages at Short Cliff. At Haven Brow the views over the Cuckmere estuary are stunning. From a stile you look down on a huge shingle beach with a lagoon behind. This is the only unspoilt river estuary in the south-east and is really magnificent.

The Way curves slightly north to a concrete plinth above the steepest section of Haven Brow, and then drops diagonally down the very eroded path to the flood embankment just to the south of the lagoon. Below you can see the remains of pill boxes that defended the Cuckmere Valley during the Second World War. The steep path is *very* slippery in wet weather.

At the bottom you pass through a gap in the fence and head west along the raised bank. The lagoon is a good site for waders, such as dunlin, ringed plover and redshank. After 550 yards (500 metres), cross the main beach track and head for the river. To the west is a salt marsh covered with rather grey, dusty-looking succulents. The Way turns north up the valley.

A little way up the valley there is a small bridge and stile across a ditch. This is the quickest route to Foxhole, where the country park camp site lies. The Way forks slightly north-westwards past the cut-off meanders **5** where the river was straightened and canalised in the 19th century.

The sheltered waters of the meanders attract dabchicks, tufted ducks and a large number of Canada geese in winter, and are popular with solitary herons and cormorants in summer. Go north to Exceat Bridge, where there is a pub and you can catch buses going either to Eastbourne or to Seaford and Brighton.

From the bridge, go east about 550 yards (500 metres) along the roadside footway to Exceat Farm. The odd orange balls hanging on the electricity lines just to the north of the main road are to stop swans flying into the wires.

Cross the road at the bus stop by the entrance to the country park, between an old granary and a cottage, to a stile marked with an acorn symbol. Among the ivy on the side of the old granary there is a South Downs Way notice. The visitor centre has an excellent exhibition on local wildlife and history, and a shop and toilets. Next door, the Living World has a marvellous series of live insect displays and tanks of marine life.

The Way heads almost north-east up the hill towards Friston Forest and at the top goes over a notch in a flint wall **B**. Turn round at this point to look down the valley back to the cut-off meanders **5** and the sea. From the waymark post, just beyond the flint stile, the path descends more than 200 steps through an archway of trees to Westdean village.

At the bottom, go past a Forestry Commission noticeboard and the village pond. After a hundred yards travelling north-east on the metalled road there is a South Downs Way concrete plinth and an acorn attached to the telegraph pole signposting the Way ahead. (A brief diversion here will take you to the village church **6**.) Head for a stile up a grass track, leading into

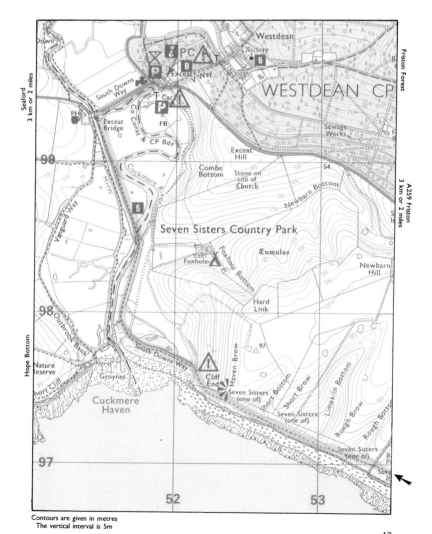

Contours are given in metres
The vertical interval is 5m

the Forestry Commission land, where there are a number of waymark posts. The aim of planting this forest was to protect locally important underground water supplies from pollution, but for the walker it is the autumn colours, winter shelter or summer shade that make it attractive. The path curves gently to the north past a waymark post by the edge of the forest, over a stile and down steps to the rear of Charleston Manor.

There is a small badger flap on the rabbit fence halfway down the steps, so that these nocturnal animals can search for food without damaging the netting. At the foot of the steps a waymark directs you along a level, beech-lined track, not quite on the definitive route. After a hundred yards turn due north over a stile beneath a cherry-plum tree. The Way now climbs alongside a ploughed field and hedge. From the top of this small hill the great arc of the Cuckmere lies to the west, below High and Over and the White Horse 7. To the north-east, Windover Hill dominates the landscape, with views up the valley to the Weald and a distant spire, which is Berwick Church.

Just before descending into Litlington past a double stile **C**, Alfriston is visible ahead on the west side of the river. You can see flint and tile cottages in the village below as you descend to a kissing gate. From here go west to the road and then north past the Plough and Harrow. Take care, as there is little or no pavement. If you wish, you can turn west and cross the river to Frog Firle Youth Hostel and buses to Alfriston and Seaford. Litlington Tea Gardens **8** are recommended for their refreshments and almost timeless atmosphere.

North of Litlington Church you have to walk on the road for approximately 275 yards (250 metres) before the Way dips off to a high roadside footpath. After 100 yards you cross a stile into a field. The definitive route runs diagonally across the fields here over a series of stiles and eventually skirts the wooded boggy patch that was once Lullington pond. As you get to the road there is a nearby stile that takes you along the eastern edge of a water meadow. You have a clear view of Alfriston Church and the white bridge. In the northern corner of the meadow a stile leads you into a small copse. After about 50 yards you join a tarmac path to meet the bridleway section of the South Downs Way. The house to the east is called Plonk Barn and the owner has thoughtfully retained the original colony of doves.

For the rest of the route in East Sussex the waymarks are blue to denote the change to bridleway status. Go over a small concrete bridge above a little chalk brook and along the path leading to the white bridge. Once on the west bank, the bridleway turns north again and past a sign saying 'horses'.

After approximately 50 yards you proceed west up River Lane towards Alfriston's square. To reach the car park and public toilets follow the signpost straight ahead through a farmyard.

The Way turns south briefly, down the High Street, and then west again between Steamer Trading and the Star Inn. Alfriston Youth Hostel is at Frog Firle, half a mile (1 km) south. You can reach it by a roadside footway or down the river-bank footpath.

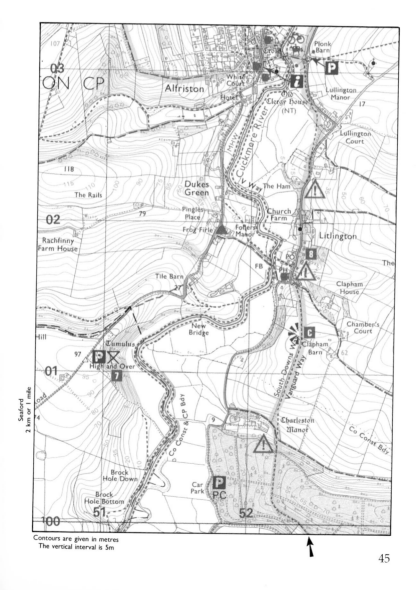

Contours are given in metres
The vertical interval is 5m

A circular walk at Beachy Head

8 miles (12.9 km)

The area between Beachy Head and Birling Gap is part of a Voluntary Marine Conservation Area, and is one of the most beautiful unspoilt environments in the Downs – a true wilderness and particularly spectacular on spring low tides when the maximum area of the chalk wave-cut platform is exposed to view.

This circular walk is made up of two loops, one between Eastbourne and Beachy Head (3 miles/4.8 km), the other near Birling Gap (2 miles/3.1 km), linked by the South Downs Way itself. You can start this walk at either end and do as much or as little as you like.

Assuming that you start from Eastbourne, head in a southerly direction past Whitebread Hole, towards Cow Gap, where there is access to the beach. As there is a risk of rock falls and rising tides, just take a quick look, then return up the steps and rejoin the circular walk. From here, continue parallel to the sea until the path turns right and heads eastwards to meet the South Downs Way.

If you intend to walk only the short loop, turn right and head back (1¼ miles/1.9 km) into Eastbourne along the national trail; otherwise, at the path junction turn left along the cliff tops towards Birling Gap. This link section (1½ miles/2.6 km) takes you past the Chalet Visitor Centre, Beachy Head lighthouse **1**,

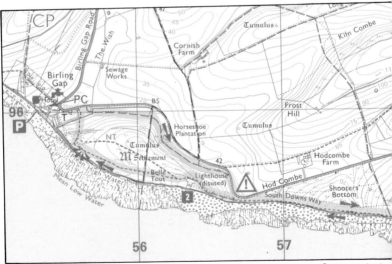

Contours are given in m
The vertical interval is

and downhill to meet the road. At this point you start the second loop.

Continue westwards along the coast, past the disused lighthouse of Belle Tout **2**, until you reach the coastguard lookout. Just past this building, turn right and walk inland towards the road. When you are on the road, you can turn left and walk into Birling Gap, where there are refreshments, or continue by turning right along the road for a few yards, then taking the next turn on to a bridleway. This runs parallel with the road, passing Horseshoe Plantation until it once again joins the road, which you follow south back to the start of this loop and the South Downs Way.

To return to Eastbourne, follow the link, now in an easterly direction, past Shooters Bottom, to rejoin the first loop at the path junction. Keep on the national trail, heading inland, back to the start of the circular walk.

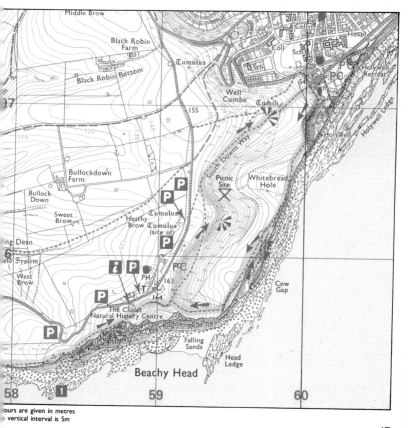

ours are given in metres
vertical interval is 5m

Beachy Head lighthouse and cliffs, seen from Belle Tout further to the west.

The Battle of Beachy Head

The Channel has seen many naval battles but in 1690, off Beachy Head, the Earl of Torrington may have invented the concept of deterrence. Commanding a combined English and Dutch fleet against the French – who believed they were supporting a Jacobite uprising – Torrington faced defeat and withdrew to the mouth of the Thames. Court-martialled for retreating, his defence was that he had maintained a 'fleet in being'. Undefeated, and still somewhere nearby, its very existence made any attempt at invasion extremely foolhardy. Two years later the French force was defeated at the battle of La Hogue.

Eastbourne

What is now mainly a seaside town was one of the first experiments in town planning. Old Town, formerly known as East Bourne, where you will find the bourne (river) to which the name refers, is a mile from the sea. Two small fishing settlements developed. Seahouses faced the beach and South Bourne lay inland from it, but the main part of the town, with open spaces and wide streets lined with trees, dates from the early 19th century. It was planned deliberately to be a pleasant place to live and to visit.

The Martello tower and the Great Redoubt also date from the Napoleonic Wars and can be visited on the way to the start of your journey.

Looking over Eastbourne, from near the eastern end of the South Downs Way, towards Pevensey Bay.

2 Eastbourne to Alfriston

Bridleway section: *through Jevington and over Windover Hill*
7½ miles (11.9 km)

(Riders usually start this bridleway section from Warren Hill car park **9** as there is nowhere suitable to un-box at the official start.)

From the signposts at Paradise Drive **A**, the official start, go up the hill in a south-westerly direction on a broad, sometimes muddy, chalk track towards woodland. About 50 yards from the start the path divides. Take the southern route, skirting the trees. You are now above the red-tiled roofs of Eastbourne and the sea lies grey-blue beyond.

A fairly gentle climb following the waymark posts takes you to the top of the Downs. You pass a silver inverted dish over a large water reservoir. It looks as if a giant spaceship has landed and been hidden here. Follow the Way in a north-westerly direction. As you rise, the views behind you, over Eastbourne, become more spectacular. There is much ash regeneration here, as this section of downland is not grazed.

The footpath crossing your route is the Jubilee Way, which runs north–south along the scarp slope. The Way is now a grassy track between thorn, bramble and fireweed. You come to a multiple junction of rides through the scrub. There is a tumulus to the north, with a flint wall adjoining, which looks like a shelter for walkers, but is actually the remains of a rare horizontal windmill **10**. Follow the waymarks directing you up the northernmost path. The grass is short here, largely due to heavy use and rabbits, and the town is obscured behind a screen of ash trees. It is still a gentle ascent, through trees stunted by the wind, with fire rides cutting across the trail at various points. The scrub thins out as you climb, until you get a view northwards along the wooded scarp edge to a circular clump above Babylon Down, known locally as Beehive Plantation.

The path curves round along the top of the scarp slope and heads north-westwards towards the A259. You pass a trig point and a dew pond hidden in the scrub. Riders coming from Warren Hill car park **9** will join the Way here. You are now on more open downland high above the town.

Just before dropping down to the road, the Way narrows. There are bus stops to the west of your crossing point. Take care, as there is a blind bend to the east. Pass the club house and head through the golf course on a broad, chalky track.

There are views down Ringwood Bottom to the suburban development of East Dean, with Friston water tower above on the skyline. The path can be 'greasy' in wet weather and uneven where the potholes have been filled with hardcore. Your route passes west of the gorse clumps at the end of the golf course. Here the Wealdway footpath, between Gravesend and Beachy Head, briefly joins the South Downs Way.

If you want to get to Beachy Head Youth Hostel **11** follow the Wealdway down the scarp slope. From this junction the trail continues for half a mile (1 km) past another maze of fire rides.

Two or three parallel routes run along the scarp top and, depending on the weather, you can choose the shelter of the scrub or the more exposed westerly path with its broader views. Where the Way just touches the head of Eldon Bottom there is a restored concrete dew pond **12** and a useful trough.

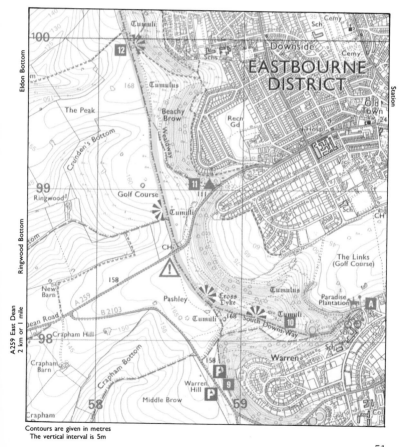

Contours are given in metres
The vertical interval is 5m

Head towards the trig point on Bourne Hill above Jevington. This is a particularly good mountain-bike run with no gates to slow you down.

Just south of the trig point the Way heads west along a flinty, sometimes muddy, track. The views are into a wide, deep, dry valley, with the village of Jevington hidden in the trees below. There is an ancient crossroads here. Old Town Eastbourne, Willingdon and Jevington are signposted on stone plinths. These look like remains from a priory or a Roman villa but are actually part of an old Barclays Bank that was bombed during the war. The Way heads westwards to Jevington down a broad track between two sheep fences. It feels like an old coach road.

To the north, you can clearly see the lynchets of a Celtic field system **13** on the side of Willingdon Bottom and Coombe Hill. There are two tracks here separated by scrub, with the Way taking the more northerly route. You can pick out the square Norman tower of Jevington Church due west as you walk down Bourne Hill, and a series of tree clumps in the fields beyond.

It is sheltered here and the wind may be less biting. Coming down the Way into Jevington, you enter an area of ash trees with dark, overhanging branches. There are rabbit holes on the south side of this path and the great, chalky, wind-blown root plates are impressive. Flint and tile cottages are visible below.

Hawthorn Lodge tea gardens (closed in winter) lie conveniently at the bottom of the track where you meet the road. At this junction, go northwards about 50 yards up the roadside and turn west again towards the church. If you are hungry or thirsty, go through the churchyard to the pub, past a tapsell gate hinged at the centre. These were designed to allow pallbearers carrying coffins to walk on either side.

At the Eight Bells, you can sit down by a fire in winter and thaw out. The row of walking boots in the entrance shows how popular the pub is with ramblers. On the way back, pause to visit the church before going north-westwards up a narrow bridleway. The fence to the south is designed to stop dogs from chasing stud horses. There are still a few elm trees here to the north of the path as you rise to Jevington Holt and Holt Brow.

The landowner has carefully fenced off the little islands of trees, which are a particular characteristic of this landscape, and hopefully they will flourish. At the western end of the special fence, you ascend more steeply underneath a canopy of trees. There is a mixture of elm, ash and horse-chestnut by the trail, but also a lot of exposed roots, so care is required at dusk.

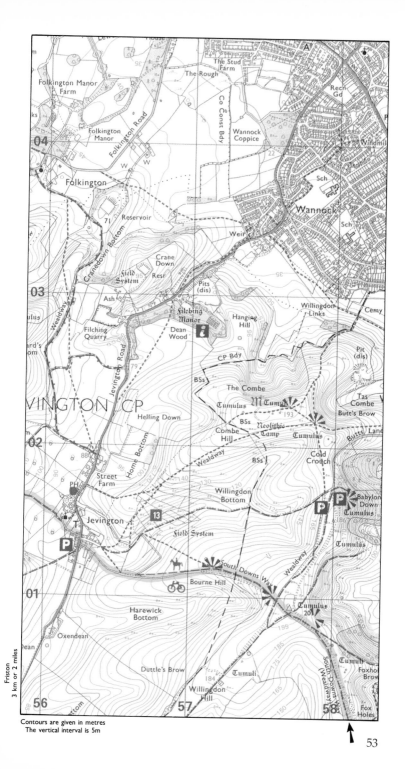

Contours are given in metres
The vertical interval is 5m

Friston
3 km or 2 miles

53

Ancient field patterns are still visible near Jevington.

About 550 yards (500 metres) out of Jevington the path levels off at a multiple bridleway junction. Your route crosses on one side of a little grass triangle to a waymark post and up a broad track beneath more trees. The Downs to the north are intensively cultivated with only a small patch of grassland remaining. Carry on westwards up to Holt Brow. As you reach higher ground, the path dries out and becomes chalkier.

On blustery days you can hear the wind beginning to roar in the trees as you gain height. At the top of the track, coming out of the woodland, there is a waymark post signalling your route north-west (right), while ahead another bridleway goes across Lullington Heath National Nature Reserve.

Pass through a narrow, scrubby section. After about 50 yards on the level you reach your first bridlegate, where the Way crosses a narrow field, with stunted ash woodland to the north-east. After 380 yards (350 metres) you come to a second gate and are effectively on a downland plateau, with views over Lullington Heath and north-west to Firle Beacon in the distance. To the north, in the centre of a very large arable field, is Hill Barn **14**, the remains of an isolated 'manure' barn. To the east you can see Beehive Plantation, the Neolithic camp at Coombe Hill, and on clear days Pevensey Bay. Notice the rabbit runs in the hedges. Head towards a post in the distance but do not be deceived by the sheep tracks.

To the south lie the 2,000 acres (800 hectares) of Friston Forest. Follow the waymarks north and then north-westwards towards the tumuli of Windover Hill. You can just see the cliffs of Newhaven and to the west the White Horse at High and Over. Before reaching Windover Hill, look south-westwards down the unspoilt dry valley of Tenantry Ground **15** and Deep Dean.

The Way passes through a wooden bridlegate and then curves round the top of Windover Hill **16** in a great arc along the route of an old coach road. The grassland is particularly good for downland flowers. From here, you can detour to the footpath above the Long Man **17**. This hill figure is best viewed from Wilmington, where there are the remains of a Benedictine priory, and a small car park with picnic site and public toilets.

The depressions on the hill top, east of the Long Man, are all that remains of some Neolithic flint mines.

Descending to the Cuckmere Valley, you go through a bridle-gate before passing the square outline of a water reservoir.

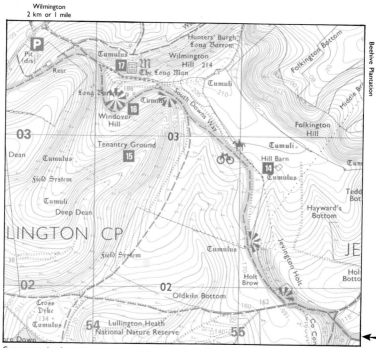

Wilmington
2 km or 1 mile

Contours are given in metres
The vertical interval is 5m

Friston Forest

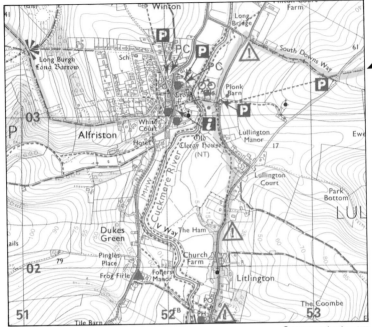

Contours are given in metres
The vertical interval is 5m

When the Way reaches the Litlington to Wilmington road, cross and continue down a wooded byway with a great arch of ash trees that offers shelter from the wind or shade from the sun. Join the Lullington to Alfriston road just east of Long Bridge.

At the bottom of this flinty track, cross another road and pass through a bridlegate in a post-and-rail fence. The Way turns southwards here, running inside the field parallel to the road towards Plonk Barn. After about 550 yards (500 metres), just off the floodplain of the River Cuckmere, proceed through another bridlegate. The bridleway and footpath sections merge here. Turn west and go over the white-painted bridge into Alfriston.

The Long Man – an historical enigma

This splendid hill figure looking 'naked to the shires' is the largest representation of a human in Western Europe.

Until its restoration, the Long Man was visible only when there was light snow on the ground, or when the sun cast shadows into its shallow depression in the chalk grassland. In 1874 a public subscription was raised through *The Times* and the figure re-cut. The outline was probably 'sanitised' by the Victorians, as there are no known neuter figures in art history!

Many theories exist as to the date and purpose of the Long Man, varying from an Iron Age agricultural fertility figure to Alfred Watkins's view that he is a 'dodman' holding two posts for surveying and establishing ley lines. He also resembles the Anglo-Saxon god Baldur, or Christian figures seen on Roman coins.

As the earliest drawings of the hill figure are from the 18th century and no proof exists one way or the other, you are left to choose whichever theory suits you. From dowsing experiments over the Man, it is more likely to be a woman!

The Long Man on Wilmington Hill.

3 Alfriston to Newmarket Inn

through Southease and Rodmell
13½ miles (21.7 km)

Before leaving Alfriston, you should visit the 14th century Clergy House – the first property to be bought by the National Trust.

From the Star pub, go up Kings Ride. At the end, the Way becomes a flinty, chalk track, a drove road along which sheep were driven to market. As you climb you occasionally get glimpses down the Cuckmere Valley to Litlington and Friston Forest beyond. Behind you in the early morning sun there is a wonderful silhouette of the Downs with Windover Hill dominating the landscape.

After a few hundred yards the Way levels off. There are smaller tracks leading to the north but your route goes straight ahead. The beautiful dry valley of France Bottom lies to the west. The track runs towards Long Burgh where it meets a multiple junction. There is a waymark post directing you ahead and then another one a little further on.

As you travel along the ridgetop, views of the Weald stretch out to the west. To the south-west is the long arc of the Comp and due south the scrub of High and Over, with the river mouth at Cuckmere Haven beyond.

The Cross Dyke shown on the map must have been long ploughed out. The Way winds gently north-westwards, rising slowly towards Bostal Hill, passing a gate and another track heading north-east. A mile and a quarter (2 km) out of Alfriston you come to a kissing gate **A**, bridleway gate and vertically slatted field entrance.

Head north-west, closer to the scarp top and past the remains of a tumulus. Below to the north-east lie the woods of Firle Estate and the huge Tithe Barn of Alciston, a shrunken medieval village. To the west you catch the first glimpses of masts on Beddingham Hill. In the far distance, to the south-west, the little white lighthouse at the entrance to Newhaven Harbour Arm is just visible on a clear day, and sometimes you will see the red funnel of the Dieppe ferry.

New Pond **18**, just to the north, and Jerry's Pond, to the south-west, are both dried-out dew ponds. Further west are more tumuli. Most of these ancient graves have been 'robbed'; you can still see where the Victorian 'digs' took place.

Round bales – symbolic of 'high tech' farming on the Downs.

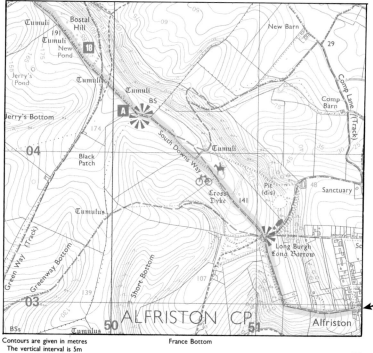

Contours are given in metres
The vertical interval is 5m

France Bottom

The Way now drops to Bopeep Bostal car park. This area is one of the favourite ridge soaring sites for local hang gliding clubs. There is a group of battered farm buildings in the dip. In the summer the undisturbed grassland on this north-facing scarp slope is a good spot for the common spotted orchid. The Way heads north-west through a post-and-rail compound, past a little weather station, and then climbs gently towards Firle Beacon **19**.

Stand on the tumulus for the best views. You can see Lewes to the north-west and Offham chalk pit beyond. On the other side of the Ouse Valley is the downland ridgetop that you will be travelling over today. Below to the north is the round Firle Tower – a folly that is a private house and part of Firle Estate, which has belonged to the Gage family since the 15th century.

From here the Way is almost level for about 2 miles (3 km). Up here it can blow so hard, and there is so little shelter, that your hands can go quite numb. To the south-west lies the bleak,

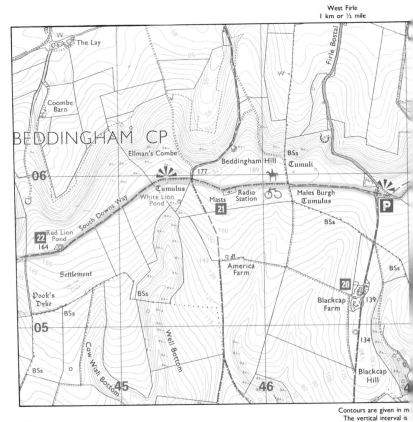

Contours are given in m
The vertical interval is

isolated Blackcap Farm **20** and the first trees you have seen on the Downs since leaving Alfriston.

At the top of Firle Bostal go through a parking area and past the square outline of a water reservoir. In January you can find ewes here with blue backsides. These coloured marks, left by the ram, tell the shepherd how efficient it has been! North is the village of Glynde, where John Ellman pioneered sheep improvement by breeding the famous Southdown in the 18th century.

Continue past the masts **21** and then north-west through a pair of bridle gates. Piddinghoe Pond, sometimes dotted with the bright sails of windsurfers, lies 2 miles (3.2 km) to the south-west. You can see the trig point next to Red Lion Pond **22** – now dried out. As you approach the brow of Itford Hill you overlook the Ouse Valley with the villages of Southease, Itford, Northease and Rodmell beyond the river. The flat brooklands, drained in the 18th century, are criss-crossed by the straight lines

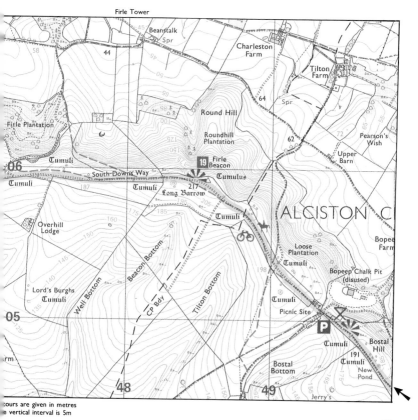

ours are given in metres
e vertical interval is 5m

of ditches. Asham pit, once a cement works, now the local tip, attracts huge flocks of scavenging seagulls. Notice the sheep tracks around the contours of the nearby steep combe. To the north you can see the square tower of Beddingham Church and, beyond, Mount Caburn with its Iron Age hill fort.

Itford Hill is an excellent place for chalk downland flowers. You might find fairy flax, salad burnet and milkwort and, if you are lucky, pyramidal, common spotted, and bee orchids.

Due west is the round tower of Southease Church and Southease bridge crossing the River Ouse. As you descend, the Way curves southwards, parallel to the river, in a large loop and at a waymark post turns back along a farm track to a bridle gate. Then go west to meet the A26 at Itford Farm. At the roadside a signpost directs you north for about 100 yards where you cross the road and pass through the farmyard. The traffic can be very heavy – so be careful! In the yard there is a water point and horse trough, specially provided by the county council as the farmer was constantly disturbed by thirsty travellers.

Just west of the farmyard is Southease station. Cross the railway line via two white, slatted gates. There are regular services – quite incredible for such a tiny halt. Go west up the tarmac road to Southease, passing over the river. The tiny bridge used to swing open for boats going upstream to Lewes. You might spot dunlin, redshank and oystercatcher feeding on the mud at low tide. Occasionally cormorants rest on posts near the water's edge and herons stalk eels or frogs in the drainage ditches.

Walkers wishing to avoid the roadside section of the Way between Southease and Rodmell can turn north along the footpath on the west bank of the river for approximately a mile (1.5 km), before turning west again along a bridleway track into Rodmell. This less hazardous route also offers the opportunity to visit Monk's House **23** (see page 71) where Virginia Woolf lived, now owned by the National Trust. Alongside Southease Church is a conveniently situated bench, an excellent place to sit and rest after the journey from Alfriston. The unusual round Saxon tower and medieval wall paintings make this a special place to visit.

To follow the roadside route from Southease, go up the hill to a waymark post by the Lewes to Newhaven road. Follow the narrow roadside path north for half a mile (1 km) to Rodmell. Riders must take great care and walkers should keep in single file. Telscombe Youth Hostel can be reached from here either by travelling up the narrow Telscombe road to the south-west, or along the safer bridleway up Cricketing Bottom, for about 2 miles (3.2 km).

At Rodmell, a waymark post directs you south-west up Mill Lane. You pass the forge with its odd collection of hoofs, metal and bones. The classical torso in a small niche above was once gilded and advertised a brand of gold paint!

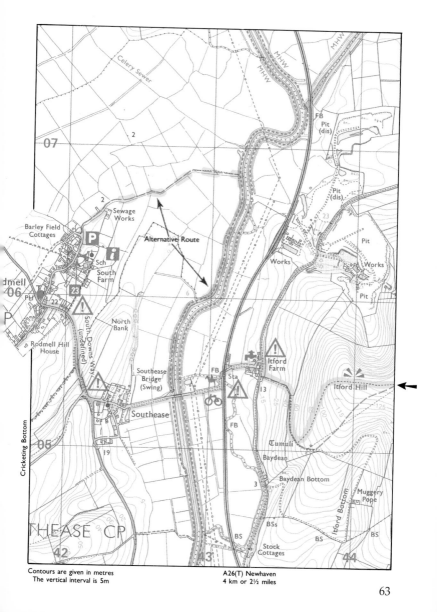

Contours are given in metres
The vertical interval is 5m

A26(T) Newhaven
4 km or 2½ miles

Looking north along the floodbanks of the River Ouse, near Southease Bridge.

As you gain height, again there are views back over the valley and on a clear day you can see the outline of Seaford Head and Haven Brow at the mouth of the Cuckmere. At the top of the hill you come to two signposts. One in yellow signals a footpath ahead, the other in blue directs you north-westwards along the Way between trees and hedges. This narrow section of path, surfaced with clinker and ash from the village forge, opens out to magnificent views along the scarp and over the Ouse Valley to Lewes. Sadly, this townscape is now dominated by the tower block of County Hall rather than the fine Norman castle. The strategic importance of Lewes can be clearly appreciated.

Continue north-westwards through a succession of bridle gates. At White Way you cross the Greenwich Meridian **24**, 0° longitude, and pass from the eastern hemisphere into the west. Beyond, the concrete track between arable fields turns westwards at a fence towards a barn on the skyline. However, you follow the waymarks east, and then north-west again, through a bridle gate along the edge of Swanborough Hill. Thirty yards north-west of a cattle trough lies a stone marked E.G. 26.12.59, a charming memorial which commemorates Mrs Greenwood, the mother of a local farmer.

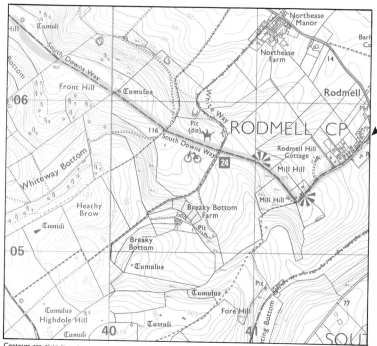

Contours are given in metres
The vertical interval is 5m

Descend gently towards Kingston Hill dew pond **25**. You can clearly see Ditchling Beacon to the north and the radio telephone mast guiding you towards Newmarket Hill. The steep sides of the scarp are another good spot for downland flowers.

Pass just to the south-west of the dew pond **25**, which has recently been restored by Northease School and South Downs Rangers. In the scrub to the east is a trough fed by water from the pond – useful for thirsty horses. A little further north-west along the Way there are two more ponds and, next to these, you pass through a metal field gate. If you want to detour to Lewes, go north-east down the scarp slope.

Overlooking the spectacular, sheep-grazed Cold Coombes to the north, the Way runs south-westwards for about half a mile (1 km). This section of the trail is part of 'Juggs Road', an ancient route used to carry fish to Lewes market. The fish were kept fresh or salted in pottery jugs – hence the name. At the gas pressure reducing station, head north-west towards the storm-damaged beeches of Newmarket plantation **26**. Here the Way turns north-east and runs a mile (1.5 km) downhill to the Newmarket Inn. There are two metal gates about 550 yards (500 metres) apart but if they are open for farm purposes this is a fantastic run for cyclists!

Lewes High Street, seen through the Norman Barbican Gate.

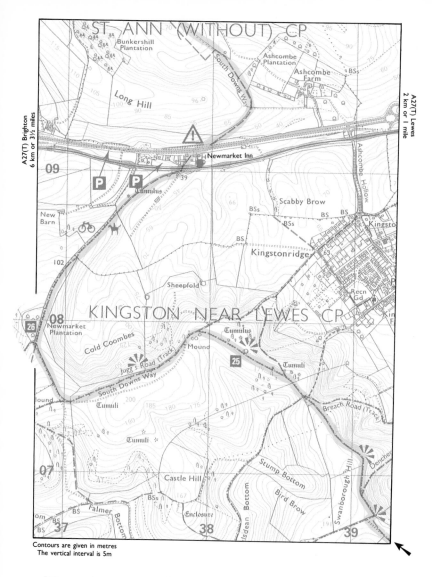

Contours are given in metres
The vertical interval is 5m

Waymark posts, at either side of a large brick arch, signal the Way under the Lewes to Brighton railway. There is a pub-restaurant and petrol filling-station here, with frequent buses to Lewes and Brighton. The Way passes between the garage and Newmarket Inn and then turns east alongside the A27 for 30 yards to a waymark post indicating the safest place to cross this dangerous dual carriageway. On the far side, you can walk into Lewes alongside the road, but it is rather noisy.

Contours are given in me
The vertical interval is 5

A CULTURAL CIRCULAR WALK OR RIDE

8¾ miles (14 km)

There are three places of interest connected with the Bloomsbury Group in this area, Berwick Church, Charleston and Monk's House. All are just a little distance from the South Downs Way.

For a circular tour to Berwick Church and Charleston come north off the South Downs Way at Long Burgh above Alfriston and curve down eastwards to Sanctuary. Here turn north again along the old Alfriston to Lewes coach road, past the recently converted Comp Barn. Just before reaching New Barn turn north-east to Berwick village and the church. After viewing the interior paintings, retrace your route to New Barn. At Alciston you might wish to divert briefly and look at the medieval tithe barn, then continue north-westwards along the coach road for 1 mile (1.5 km), before turning north-east to Tilton Farm. From here, turn west along a concrete farm track to Charleston Farm. Do not miss its beautifully kept garden.

From Charleston, continue westwards just south of Firle Tower folly to Heighton Street. From here turn south to rejoin the old coach road, briefly west again for about 200 yards and then up the scarp slope to rejoin the South Downs Way. There are car parks at Bopeep picnic site, Alfriston, Charleston and a very small one at Berwick Church, where you could start this circular trip. The whole route is a bridleway, so riders, walkers and cyclists can enjoy it.

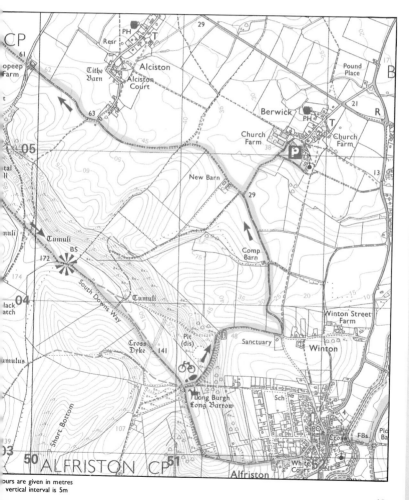

ours are given in metres
vertical interval is 5m

The Bloomsbury Group in Sussex

The Bloomsbury Group was a group of English writers, artists and philosophers who met between 1907 and 1930 in the Bloomsbury district of London to discuss aesthetic and philosophical questions. Nearly all had been at Trinity or King's College, Cambridge. Members of the group included Leonard and Virginia Woolf, writers and founders of the Hogarth Press; Clive Bell and Roger Fry, the art critics; Duncan Grant and Vanessa Bell, the painters; Lytton Strachey, the biographer; and Maynard Keynes, the economist.

Berwick Church

The Church of St Michael and All Angels at Berwick contains extensive decorative work by Vanessa Bell, Quentin Bell and Duncan Grant. The small rectangular interior is dominated by the rich and flowing colours of four major murals, the characteristic flower-motif pulpit and numerous smaller paintings in the loose and direct 'Bloomsbury style'. They were commissioned in 1941 and installed with some opposition to their 'modern' nature. Much use was made of local figures and settings. A soldier and airman from Firle and a sailor from Berwick kneel respectfully. The Nativity scene is set in Tilton barn with Firle Beacon in the background.

Charleston farmhouse, Firle

Charleston farmhouse was 'discovered' by Virginia and Leonard Woolf in 1916 and was subsequently rented by Virginia's sister Vanessa Bell as a country retreat. For decades it was to be occupied by painters and writers of the Bloomsbury Group. Life was unconventional and bohemian, an outpost of cultural and intellectual activity in a remote part of the Sussex countryside.

Charleston is unique for its remarkable interior. It houses the most important remaining domestic work of painters Vanessa Bell and Duncan Grant. Textiles, pottery, carpets and wall paintings adorn each room with their characteristic flower and figure motifs.

With the death of the last tenant, Duncan Grant, in 1978, aged 93, the house was left in a sad state of repair. The Charleston Trust was formed to purchase, restore and preserve the house, its contents and garden for the future. It was opened to the public in the summer of 1986.

(Open April to the end of October on Wednesdays, Thursdays, Saturdays, Sundays and Easter and Bank Holiday Mondays, 2–6 p.m. (last admission 5 p.m.) price £3 (concession for children, OAPs, unwaged, students). April, May and October or midweek £2.25. Tel. Ripe (032 183) 265.)

Monk's House, Rodmell

Monk's House **23** was the home of Leonard and Virginia Woolf from 1919. Located on the winding village street, it is a modest brick and flint dwelling, now owned by the National Trust, with a rambling garden backing on to the walls of the churchyard. From this house Virginia, overcome by mental illness, walked towards the River Ouse and her suicide in 1941. The small, low rooms contain examples of the decorative work of Vanessa Bell and Duncan Grant in the form of painted tiled fireplaces, decorated furniture and ceramics.

(Open May to September 2–6 p.m., October 2–5 p.m., Wednesdays and Saturdays; £1.20.)

Lewes

Lewes's name derives from the Anglo-Saxon word *hlaew*, meaning hill, and there has been a settlement here since Roman times. The town dominates the strategic downland gap cut by the River Ouse. All roads, railways and canalised sections of river pass this point.

The Saxons established a coin mint to encourage trade by land and water and this commercial function was reinforced by the Normans, who built the town's castle and priory.

In 1264 the King of England, Henry III, was defeated by Simon de Montfort at the Battle of Lewes and one of the first representative parliaments was established. The town later stood for religious freedom, and local Protestants were burned at the stake (now celebrated on 5th November). In the 18th century Tom Paine developed his republican views in the debating club at the White Hart and went on to write *The Rights of Man*.

To wander the streets looking at architecture ranging from Saxon to Georgian, and to explore the narrow 'twittens', is a relaxing change from tramping the bare downland. The town has a good variety of shops and places of interest, but perhaps its association with political freedom links it to the experience of travelling the Way. On a less sophisticated note the town's brewery, Harveys, makes fantastic beer!

4 Newmarket Inn to Pyecombe

past Ditchling Beacon and Clayton Windmills
8½ miles (13.5 km)

Cross the A27 just east of the Newmarket Inn to a waymark post on the north side of the road. Take great care. Turn north-east and go up a narrow incline. Pass through a bridle gate adjoining the roadside woodland.

After rising gently for 550 yards (500 metres) the Way enters a wood by a bridle gate and stile, then runs alongside a flint wall. Here, in Ashcombe Plantation **27**, take care as you pass torn-out root plates. The path curves north-west within the wood. On leaving the plantation you can see the remains of a dew pond in the dip below.

At the bottom of the dip the route is waymarked to the north-west up a grassy headland and a long gentle climb to the scarp. Looking back to the south-east you can see Firle Beacon and a long silhouette of the scarp slope to Itford Hill. To the north you can see the tree clump of Blackcap, below which lies the woodland of Ashcombe Bottom. There is no real need for fences in this arable landscape. Gates standing in isolation and old dew ponds act as reminders that there used to be stock here. To the west and north-west the sun casts shadows on the ridgelines of the huge Celtic field system of Balmer Down **28**. Here the Way has 'drifted' significantly from the definitive route. Follow the stony track towards the pylons.

About 100 yards after passing under the electricity lines the Way turns north at a waymark post, and after about 60 yards it is flanked by a thorn hedge. On the western side of the path is an

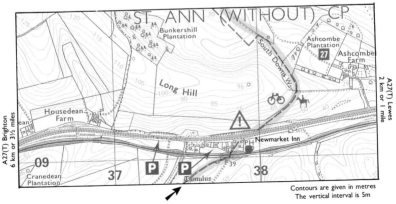

Contours are given in metres
The vertical interval is 5m

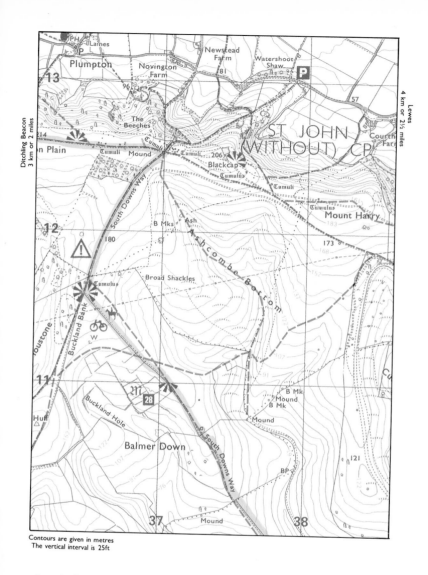

Contours are given in metres
The vertical interval is 25ft

electric fence and obviously riders should take care. To the east you can see the converted grandstand of old Lewes Racecourse.

As you pass alongside the large rectangular plantation, you will feel the benefit of its shelter. The trees on the fringes survived the great storm of 1987, whereas those in the centre were flattened.

The Way turns sharply west along the ridgetop to Ditchling Beacon. There is a waymark here. Travellers going east could divert to Lewes. You now start to get magnificent panoramas.

From Plumpton Plain the Way gently descends to Streathill Farm. In the scrub and trees to the south-west is a Bronze Age settlement **29**. You can look down to Ditchling and Westmeston. Note how wooded the landscape of the clay Weald is, compared with the Downs. Just before reaching Streathill Farm a stony track leads down to the Half Moon pub and camp site near Plumpton racecourse.

North of the farm, the Way goes west across a tarmac road cut deeply into the Downs, and through a bridle gate. This is a sheltered spot to sit and have a drink. In summer, it is a particularly good site for common spotted orchids. You might also notice lots of snails here. These animals, which need chalk to make their shells, are found in large numbers on old, unploughed downland.

The route runs through a long narrow grassland field. Just over the edge of the scarp slope you can see the tree tops forming part of a woodland 'V' **30** planted to commemorate Queen Victoria's Silver Jubilee in 1887.

Beyond Western Brow you pass an ancient deep track, and 550 yards (500 metres) further on there is a dried-out dew pond south of your route, just before you reach the Ditchling Beacon road. Cross with particular care, as people drive up this small country lane far too fast. Go through the National Trust car park, where there is often a welcome ice-cream vendor.

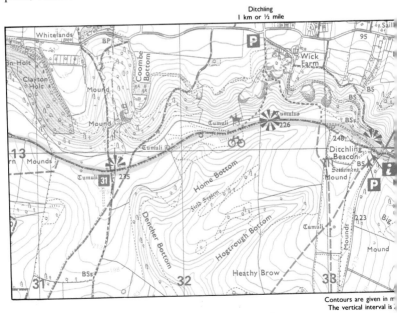

Ditchling
1 km or ½ mile

Contours are given in m
The vertical interval is

South of the main car park lie the ploughed-out remains of an Iron Age fort. In the north-western corner is an information board with details of a circular walk network.

Just to the west the Sussex Wildlife Trust has a nature reserve. You are free to wander down the slope to look at the flowers and butterflies. Of particular interest are likely to be orchids, including burnt, fragrant, frog, musk and bee. Sadly, the botanical interest of this chalk grassland site is declining because of lack of grazing, and the area is therefore being invaded by scrub.

There is a trig point in the centre of the hill fort and a viewing plinth, from which vandals have stolen the brass direction finder. You can see west to Wolstonbury Hill, beyond to Devil's Dyke, and on a clear day as far as Chanctonbury Ring.

From this high point you gently descend towards Keymer Post **31**. The Way here has an open feel. There are constant views northwards to Burgess Hill and the densely populated area of mid-Sussex. On leaving the reserve, the Way continues on the level westwards, past the remains of two neglected dew ponds. By the westernmost pond, go through a bridle gate. It can be very muddy here where the cattle have 'puddled' the ground. Climb gently through an arable field on a broad track.

At the brow of the hill is another bridle gate. Just to the west you reach the remains of Keymer Post **31** – hopefully to be restored! Here, you pass into West Sussex. You can just see the

B2116 Ditchling
2 km or 1 mile

ours are given in metres
vertical interval is 25ft

sails of one of the 'Jack and Jill' windmills **32** peeping above the skyline, and Wolstonbury Hill almost isolated from the rest of the downland, with dry valleys on either side.

After half a mile (1 km) turn sharply south through New Barn Farm. Here it is worth a detour to visit Clayton Windmills **32**. 'Jack' is privately owned; 'Jill', the small white post mill, is open, but only on summer Sundays. About 100 yards beyond the farm turn west again. In the deep dry valley below you can see Pyecombe. In autumn there are hundreds of rooks feeding on the stubble – a spectacular sight, but noisy. The collective name for rooks is, appropriately, a 'clamour'.

You no longer find the blue bridleway symbol now you are in West Sussex, even though you are still on a bridleway . Here the main indicators of the route are oak fingerposts. The Way continues westwards through a bridle gate alongside Pyecombe Golf Course. This track can be heavily cut up by horses and is obviously very well used. Near the club house the Way passes the car park and drops to the road. Cross carefully. The trail then runs south behind a thorn hedge. This is a very narrow, rough-surfaced section – difficult for riders. At a fingerpost you go south-west into Pyecombe village along School Lane. Riders and walkers should take care as there is no pavement.

Looking towards Chanctonbury – Edburton Hill motte and bailey.

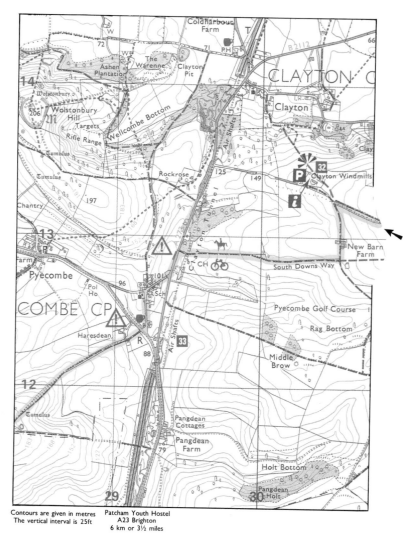

Contours are given in metres
The vertical interval is 25ft

Patcham Youth Hostel
A23 Brighton
6 km or 3½ miles

Pyecombe has a square, squat-towered, Norman church. The inside is very plain but with an unusual lead font. From the church turn south down Church Lane. You can see the circular air shaft towers **33** of the London to Brighton railway to the east as you pass down the lane towards the pub. At last you reach the Plough Inn, which welcomes walkers, even in muddy boots. *Immense* care should be taken crossing the main road. The bus stop to Brighton (15 minutes) is just south of the main traffic lights. Patcham Youth Hostel is 2 miles (3 km) away, on the road to Brighton.

From Newtimber Hill the downs-foot village of Poynings can be made out, with

...leigh Hill in the background.

5 Pyecombe to Upper Beeding

Passing Devil's Dyke and Tottington Barn Youth Hostel
6¾ miles (10.9 km)

Start from the Plough Inn. Crossing the fast A23 is very dangerous, particularly for horses. There is a fingerpost pointing you westwards up a concrete track past Brendon's Riding School. Continue through a metal bridle gate and past a nearby water trough. Start climbing the hill from this point up a broad chalk and flint track. The traffic noise can still be quite loud here, but there are fine views back towards the squat tower of Pyecombe Church and the windmills beyond.

There are two farm tracks (not shown on the map) leading off to the south and west; the Way curves up the hill in a south-westerly direction. There are a number of deep ruts alongside the route, which indicate that it has been used for hundreds of years, perhaps as a drover's road. Higher up, there are signs of gulley erosion with the bedrock of chalk exposed where the topsoil has been washed away.

Pass through a metal bridle gate next to a field gate halfway up the hill, and proceed to a fingerpost on the horizon. Looking back the views are tremendous. You can see the flat-topped outline of the quarry spoil heaps on Wolstonbury Hill. Numerous mountain-bike tracks indicate the growing popularity of this hobby.

A dew pond shown on the map is buried in scrub to the east. The Way has drifted from the definitive route here, but you still head in a westerly direction along the main track. There is another smaller track straight ahead, which is not marked as a right of way on the map. To the south you can just see the tower blocks of Brighton and the coastal conurbations.

At the summit of West Hill there is an oak fingerpost next to a metal bridle gate. Westwards lies the deep dry valley of Devil's Dyke (see map on page 83) and in the distance the three masts on Truleigh Hill. Pass through the gate and drop down towards Saddlescombe Farm. The pasture underfoot is pleasant to walk on, less sticky than bare ground in the winter and softer going for horses. At the western corner of this field, where you meet another bridleway coming from the south, curve down to the farm through a wooden bridle gate and along a narrow, wooded track. The path deepens, and at the bottom of the track you pass a National Trust signpost for Newtimber Hill. Go through another bridle gate on to a short section of the route, which is heavily used by cattle and can be very muddy, then take the harder, drier track avoiding the farmyard.

As you pass the green and cream farmworkers' cottages you may spot a little hand-painted sign saying 'gloves £1.00 a pair'. Clearly the demand from cold winter walkers on the South Downs Way has led to this enterprising sideline! The farm building, which looks like a granary, houses a donkey wheel that was used as the power-source for the farm. If you ask you may be able to look at this interesting relic – like a giant hamster's exercise wheel!

Back on the Way there are a number of faded fingerposts pointing through the hamlet. The track descends to the road and another narrow wooden bridle gate. Care should be taken crossing the road here, as the traffic is fast.

Go up the steep, flinty track past a large ash tree. About 100 yards from the road the main track curves sharply round to the south-west, past the reservoir with an iron-railing fence. The definitive route of the South Downs Way goes to the south but is so badly waymarked and overgrown as to be impassable. Gently climb the hill through a scrubby area into a rutted grass

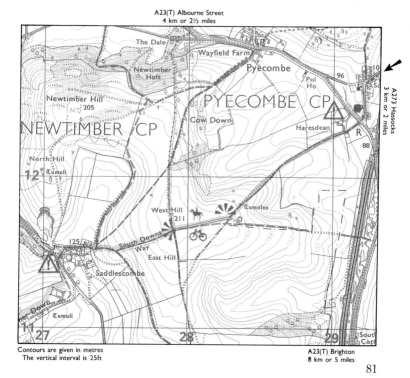

Contours are given in metres
The vertical interval is 25ft

car park. The Way westwards is not at all clear. Carry on in a south-westerly direction and decide which of the tracks to take. The one nearest the road is the route indicated on the map. The alternative parallel track to the north is the best one to take at present, as the definitive route is far too narrow and overgrown for horses.

Near the top of the hill you overlook the impressive deep dry valley of the Devil's Dyke **34**. (Why not make a brief diversion to explore its flora and butterflies?) This is a long, gentle climb and you can just see the trig point through the thorn trees.

The Way meets the road leading to the hotel but crosses to a wooden bridleway gate. It is worth a walk up the roadside path to the Dyke Hotel, either for refreshments or for the stunning views. Inside the pub there are some interesting old photographs of the area: there used to be an aerial ropeway crossing the Dyke, a steam railway coming up from Brighton, and the place was more popular in Victorian times than it is today!

The deep dry valley of Devil's Dyke was probably cut when the ground was permanently frozen in the Ice Age.

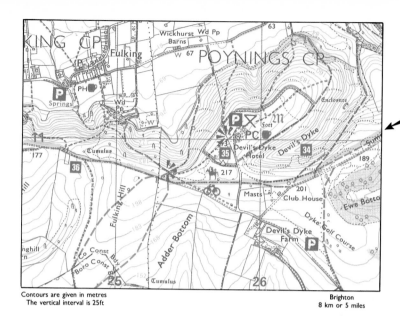

Contours are given in metres
The vertical interval is 25ft

Brighton
8 km or 5 miles

The quality of the views over the Weald varies from brilliant clarity to an eerie, low-lying mist clothing the landscape. The scarp slope stretches to the west and below lies the village of Fulking, with its sheep-washing spring dedicated to Ruskin. There are often colourful groups of hang gliders and para-gliders preparing to take off.

Rejoin the South Downs Way heading westwards towards the masts on Truleigh Hill. Go past the fingerpost in the middle of the level field and carry on westwards to the corner, where you pass through a bridle gate. The Devil's Dyke Iron Age fort **35**, which took advantage of the natural features, is best viewed from here.

From Fulking Hill you can see the Way undulating and winding westwards, and can just catch glimpses of Edburton Church at the foot of the Downs. This is an excellent stretch for mountain bikers.

The pylons march across the Downs here – hopefully one day the electricity lines will be put underground. Above Fulking you meet a number of deeply cut bridleways coming up the scarp slope. Next to the fence is a large lump of calcite that has been ploughed up by the farmer – one of the few crystals found on the Downs. The little scrubby area in the field to the south marks the remaining foundations of Fulking Isolation Hospital **36**, used for people with contagious diseases.

83

Looking past Anchor Bottom towards the patchwork landscape of the Adur Valley from Beeding Hill.

From Perching Hill at 580 feet (177 metres) you descend steeply under the powerline that crosses this notch in the Downs and heads up towards Edburton Hill. It is just possible to see the remaining outline of a motte and bailey castle **37** on the skyline. Just as you pass under the line there is a metal bridle gate adjoining a field gate. A sign indicates that the National Trust owns Fulking Escarpment, which is an excellent site for downland flowers and insects.

The Way is now a broad, flinty track through huge arable fields rising gently around the south side of Edburton Hill. The lack of background noise, and the open treeless landscape, allow sounds to carry great distances. Curve down to a second notch in the Downs above Edburton village, where the views to the north are rediscovered but lost again when you start to climb Truleigh Hill.

The fields are almost 'perfectly' managed – there is not a blade of barley or wheat out of place. At the edge of the scarp there is a fingerpost and a further National Trust sign. Bridleways lead down the escarpment and it is worth diverting briefly to look at the chalk grassland, which contrasts with nearby 'high tech' farming. This low spot offers some shelter.

Then you begin to climb Truleigh Hill. The Way passes just to the south of Truleigh Hill Barn and alongside a cluster of buildings, sheds and fences. The views are south towards the coastal sprawl of Shoreham and Worthing. It is so bleak here that newly planted trees struggle to grow.

From Freshcombe Farm you have a gentle downhill run into the valley of the River Adur. Just below the brow of the hill is Tottington Barn Youth Hostel, surrounded by pines. Although it looks like a landscaped office block, it is actually a converted 1930s summer house. There is a water point here. Bed and breakfast and evening meals are available, and the hostel is well equipped and offers a vegetarian menu.

Just to the west, the track becomes metalled and is a fast downhill run for cyclists, although a bridleway running parallel to the Way provides a softer route for horses.

Contours are given in metres
The vertical interval is 25ft

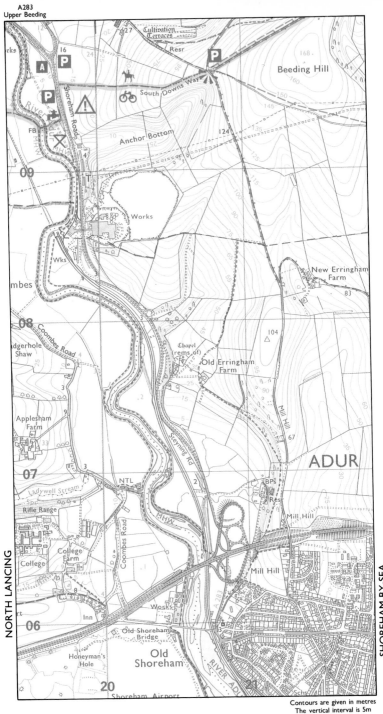

Cultivation Terraces

Resr

168

Beeding Hill

160

South Downs Way

150

145

Anchor Bottom

124

135

125

09

Works

100

Wks

80

75

65

New Erringham Farm

83

08

Coombes Road

Badgerhole Shaw

104

Chapel (rems of)

Old Erringham Farm

90

Applesham Farm

Mill Hill

67

07

NTL

ADUR

BP

Resr

Ladywell Stream

Rifle Range

Mill Hill

Mill Hill

NORTH LANCING

College Farm

College

SHOREHAM-BY-SEA

06

Inn

Works

A283

Old Shoreham Bridge

Honeyman's Hole

Old Shoreham

RIVER ADUR

20

Shoreham Airport

21

Schurs

Contours are given in metres
The vertical interval is 5m

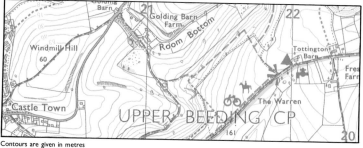

Contours are given in metres
The vertical interval is 25ft

There are sheep on the Downs here. The views westwards can be obscured by mist but, on a good day, are quite superb and you can clearly see the clump of trees at Chanctonbury Ring. The contrast between the valley and the Downs makes these hills feel quite mountainous. As you reach Beeding Hill the sound of traffic intrudes again. The chimney stack of the cement works peers over the line of the Downs, and to the south the chapel of Lancing College reaches skywards, its Gothic spires just visible.

Just below Beeding Hill and a mile (1.5 km) west of the youth hostel, there is a six-way path junction and a small car park next to a large South Downs Way fingerpost, erected in 1973 by the Society of Sussex Downsmen. Sadly, one of the arms has been damaged. Do not follow the main track here, but pass through a rather rickety bridle gate where a second fingerpost signs the Way ahead into a large pasture field. The Way runs south-west near a deep dry valley called Anchor Bottom. You can see the shadows cast by the meadow ant hills on the far side of this valley, and ridges created by the cattle walking around the contours. Below lies the River Adur in its flood embankment, not far from the roundabout **A** and traffic of the A283. The Way continues through a large metal field gate. Descend gradually into the valley on a chalky track with fenced arable fields on either side. At Castle Town, you can see a mock medieval château, which is actually a convent school. Note that the bypass for Steyning, Bramber and Upper Beeding is not yet marked on all maps.

Where the Way meets the main road, go southwards towards the little bridleway bridge over the River Adur.

From here there are buses going both north and south. These are 'request' stops, so remember to indicate to the driver by waving your hand that you wish him to stop.

Dew ponds – a downland enigma

As you travel along the ridgetop of the high, dry Downs you occasionally pass shallow, saucer-like depressions of either puddled clay, chalk or concrete, which are the damp or dried-out remains of 'dew ponds'. In the heyday of downland sheep farming, before the invention of plastic water piping, there were literally thousands of these ponds between Beachy Head and Winchester. Their purpose was to supply drinking water for sheep, but an elaborate mythology has developed around them, because few people were able to understand why they often held water in even the driest summers.

The name 'dew pond' is recent. Over 150 years ago they were called 'sheep ponds', 'mist ponds', 'fog ponds', or 'cloud ponds', and these hint at their true nature.

The first of the ponds may have been made by people who noticed that chalk or clay that had been trampled by cattle became watertight. The majority are lined with clay, to which a little quicklime was added to stop worm damage. Some ponds had straw mixed with the clay to reduce cracking in summer, and many had a layer of flints to protect the clay from penetration by animals' feet. All in all they are a fascinating and quite sophisticated piece of early engineering and, as the price of plastic piping rises and sheep are returned to the Downs, we may see more being reconstructed.

In the early 20th century, Edward A. Martin was given a grant by the Royal Geographical Society to undertake a series of experiments to discover the true source of supply to these ponds. Prior to these studies, which lasted more than three years, people believed that the ponds were replenished each night by dew. Interestingly, Martin found that there were very few occasions when the surface of the ponds was below dew-point and thus capable of condensing any airborne moisture. In fact, he estimated that the maximum annual dew-fall on the Downs does not exceed 1.5 inches (3.8 cm). Clearly, the main supply of water is from rain! The average annual rainfall on the high ridge of the Downs is 35 inches (89 cm), and the evaporation of water from the surface of the pond is approximately 18 inches (46 cm), giving a net gain of 17 inches (43 cm) over the whole area. And when rain falls on the edge of the pond some percolates into the ground and some adds to the water.

If you look at the shape of dew ponds, you can see that the actual rainfall collecting area is very large relative to the smaller evaporation surface. Martin inspected many ponds to see how they were constructed, and even built an experimental pond to see if it was possible to insulate the clay lining from the warming influence of the ground. He clearly proved that dew had almost nothing to do with filling these ponds. He also disproved the myth that they never dry up. He concluded that the rolling sea mists, low clouds and fogs of summer came to their rescue and helped to fill the pond a little and, more significantly, to reduce the evaporation. Even in 1910 he bemoaned the fact that because farmers took them for granted, their failure to maintain them often led to cracking and plant-growth damage, so that the ponds dried up.

Nowadays, the few that still function, such as those on Lullington Heath and Kingston Hill, have been restored by conservationists.

A dew pond on Newtimber Hill – surprisingly, it still holds water.

6 Upper Beeding to Washington

via Steyning Bowl and past Chanctonbury Ring
6¾ miles (10.9 km)

There is a small car park at the roundabout **A** on the Upper Beeding road. From a layby on the A283 the trail passes through a rather ramshackle metal field gate. Beyond this go south, parallel to the main road, and then turn westwards between post-and-rail fencing to a bridle-bridge over the river. At this point there is a picnic area, trough and drinking fountain provided by the Society of Sussex Downsmen, but the water is turned off in winter.

The river has tidal flood banks either side with footpaths on top. Historically it was an important trade link and in the medieval period Bramber, one mile (1.5 km) upstream, was a significant port. The town even produced coinage.

At the other side of the bridge, go north-west alongside the river. Just to the west you can see the little church of Botolphs **38**. This is Saxon and lies in a hamlet near a timber-framed clergy house. The church has a Horsham stone roof and the hamlet is so small, it is indicative of a shrunken medieval village. The Way leaves the bank at a fingerpost and crosses the floodplain of the River Adur on a raised bridleway. Watch out for cormorants feeding in the river and drainage ditches.

Just before the road there is a tourist information sign and a fingerpost indicating the Way westwards, while the Downs Link path runs north along a disused railway line – and links the North Downs Way with the South Downs Way. Go through a metal bridle gate adjoining a field gate and follow the road in a north-westerly direction. The verge is quite narrow, so riders should take care. Curve westwards and pass through Annington Farm as you start to climb the western slopes of the Adur Valley. About 50 yards past Mulberry 'Cottage' the Way turns south and leaves the tarmac.

Go up a broad farm drive with sycamore, ash and elm making a fine arch of trees in the summer. At 'Tinpotts' there is a South Downs Way fingerpost directing you a little further to the south, and then another one pointing south-westwards.

Start climbing up the Downs along a sunken, wooded lane towards a metal bridle gate. There are distinctive blocks of trees planted in the dry valley of Winding Bottom, as well as a line of pylons. Head north-westwards, past a burnt-out modern barn, through a gate system which looks as though it is rarely closed. To the east you can see the cement works, and the River Adur meandering down to the sea.

The landscape is a mixture of arable and pasture, and the track is quite flinty ahead. As you climb there are views to the south and east over this beautiful valley. Follow the north side of the fence, as it curves round to head in a westerly direction. You start to get views over the upper Adur Valley and Weald. Below lies Bramber, with its Norman castle which was still of strategic importance during the Civil War in 1643.

The Downs are bare here, giving a sense of isolation. Approaching the western end of the field above Winding Bottom you can just see the road that leads from Bramber to Steyning around the head of Steyning Bowl. At a bridle gate the Way is signposted northwards. Follow the directions shown by the fingerpost, not the old route indicated on the map. Go west past Bramber Beeches **39**, a group of trees planted by the West Sussex Federation of Women's Institutes, and follow the fence line. There are splendid views into Steyning Bowl **40** (see map on page 93), a huge, dry valley or combe sometimes used for hang gliding.

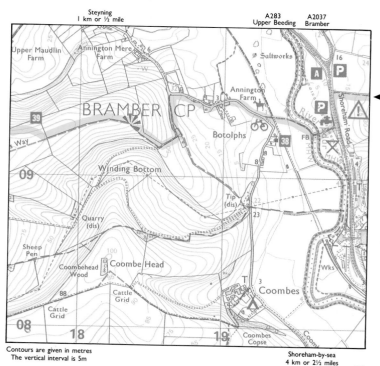

Contours are given in metres
The vertical interval is 5m

While quite pleasant underfoot for horses, this section could probably be a little scary for riders if noisy model aircraft are being flown. At the end of the fence you turn south briefly and then go through a wooden bridle gate. From here carry on westwards, with the fence again on your north side. This open landscape is a good spot for a gallop past the gaunt outlines of wind-blown trees. When you reach the brow of the hill and join the road there are broad views westwards.

The Way heads north up a verge-side path that is sometimes full of molehills. To the west, across a dry valley, you can see the ramparts of Cissbury Ring, which incorporates an Iron Age hill fort and Neolithic flint mines. The Downs feel plateau-like and can be very cool on a windy day. The verge narrows and you have to ride or walk carefully up the road. There is a picnic site, car park and hang gliding spot at Steyning Bowl **40**, with splendid views east to Truleigh Hill.

At a point where the road turns north-eastwards the Way is signposted through a metal field gate. Great care is required in crossing the road. The Way then becomes a farm track heading towards a clump of scrub on the skyline. Go north across an arable field to another metal gate. At a multiple bridleway junction the route is signposted towards a trig point. The Way here is a flinty track. As you approach the scarp edge you can see northwards to villages in the Weald. All the woodland clumps look ragged from the great 1987 storm and the slope is clothed in trees rather than downland grass.

From the trig point, if you wish, you could make a diversion down to Steyning to pick up supplies and visit this charming Saxon village, once a port, until the silting up of the River Adur in the 13th century. Steyning became popular this century with writers and artists – William Butler Yeats and James Whistler both stayed here.

Also from the trig point you have a long, ridgetop run ideal for mountain bikers and riders. Ahead to the west you can see the clump of beech trees which marks the Chanctonbury Ring Iron Age hill fort. On the bitterest winter days you can still meet parties of hardy local ramblers enjoying the fresh air, even singing Christmas carols as they walk along! Looking southwards down the dry Steyning Valley there are better views of Cissbury Ring in the distance.

At the westernmost head of the Steyning Valley there are the remains of a dried-out dew pond **41** with ash and thorn trees growing in its bed.

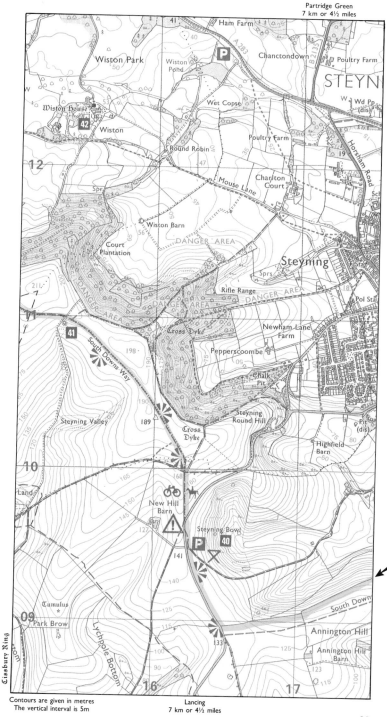

Wiston Park

P

Ham Farm

Chanctondown

Poultry Farm

STEYN

Wiston Pond

Wet Copse

W

Wd Pp
(dis)

Wiston House

53

Wiston

Round Robin

Poultry Farm

19

Horsham Road

Mouse Lane

Charlton
Court

Sch

12

Spr

Wiston Barn

DANGER   AREA

Court
Plantation

Steyning

211

Rifle Range

Sprs

DANGER   AREA

DANGER   AREA

Pol Sta

11

41

South Downs Way

Cross Dyke

DANGER   AREA

Newham Lane
Farm

Pepperscoombe

198

Chalk
Pit

190

Steyning Valley

189

Cross
Dyke

Steyning
Round Hill

Pit
(dis)

Highfield
Barn

10

168

New Hill
Barn

Steyning Bowl

Land

P

40

Tumulus

141

Park Brow

140

South Down

Annington Hill

09

Tissbury Ring

125

Annington Hill
Barn

123

Lychpole Bottom

90

133

115

16

17

Wiston House, near Steyning, is visible from the South Downs Way.

You can see Stump Barn ahead and the outline of Chanctonbury Ring **43** on the skyline to the north-west. On reaching the finger of woodland running up from Stump Barn, you come to another signpost. You may notice some chestnut sheep hurdles here, leaning against the fence – a traditional Wealden woodland product sold to the downland shepherds. Stump Barn, despite its splendid name, is actually a modern building.

You pass a sheep-penning area by Lion's Bank, where the shepherd will mark and count his flock. You can just see Wiston House **42** (see map on page 95) and the surrounding parkland through the trees in winter. There is a multiple bridleway junction at the top of the storm-damaged Chalkpit Wood and a fingerpost directs you towards Chanctonbury Ring **43**. The Way climbs gently from here to 780 feet (238 metres) at the high point of Chanctonbury Hill, just a little west of the Ring.

It is difficult to make out the cross dyke and tumulus mentioned on the map as you pass through a wooden bridle gate beside a cattle grid. Many of the archaeological features mapped in the 1960s have been further damaged by continued arable farming.

The South Downs Way now curves gently to the south of Chanctonbury Ring **43**, famous for its clump of beech trees planted in 1760 by the young Charles Goring of Wiston. It is said that for months he carried water up the hill in bottles to aid their growth. When some of these trees blew over in the 1987 storm they revealed interesting Iron Age and Roman archaeological features and the site will be properly excavated before any major replanting. There are magnificent views all around from this vantage point. Sometimes the mists below are thick enough to mislead children into thinking they are looking out over the sea.

Travelling west again you can see the trig point of Chanctonbury Hill and the edge of a dew pond to the south. It is worth a brief diversion to the high spot to look north-west. Down below, at the scarp foot, you can see the contrasting geology of the sand pit at Rock Common.

Rejoin the trail and take the main track southwards towards Findon, passing through a bridle gate next to a cattle grid. Have a quick look at the dew pond, which was originally constructed around 1870 and has now been restored by the Society of Sussex Downsmen, then head along the main track, with the deep valley of Well Bottom to the south. Curve southwards to a fingerpost where you turn north-west.

The trail now descends with fences either side, and you see large sheep flocks grazing, rather than ploughed arable Downs. At the scarp foot lies Washington and you can begin to hear the traffic of the A24. Where the track winds its way into woodlands, you pass wayfaring trees, elder, hazel coppice and some oaks. Mountain bikers have to brake hard on the bends going down this steep, flinty track.

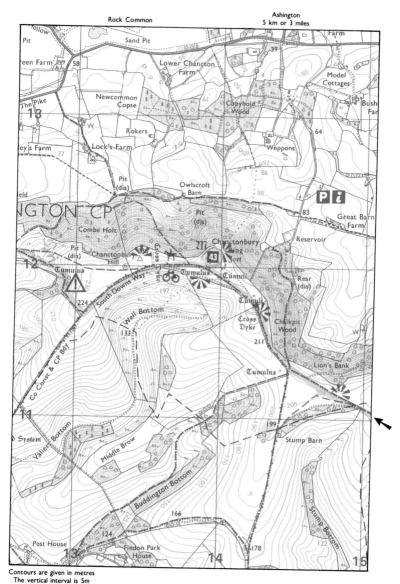

Contours are given in metres
The vertical interval is 5m

As you come out of the little wood there is some good chalk grassland to the north. Past the deserted farmhouse at Frieslands there is old man's beard on the bushes and garden escapes of cotoneaster among the natural downland species. The ground can be very sticky in winter, with your boots carrying large clods. Horses are best led.

On the descent you pass a gas pressure-reducing station, the noise and smell of which bring you back to 'civilisation'. At the bottom of the hill is an excellent car park and tourist information point.

Just beyond, the Way is signposted south to the A24, where it joins the little loop road to Washington. Do not take the track to the quarry. The trail goes directly across the dual carriageway here and great care should be taken.

There are buses running north and south and it is a short walk up the side road to Washington. By taking this route, riders can avoid the dangerous crossing. At the village turn west, go past the church and across a bridge over the A24. Continue to Rowdell House, where you turn briefly south **B** and then southwest up the scarp slope to rejoin the South Downs Way at Barnsfarm Hill.

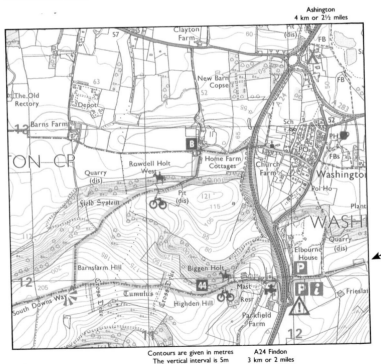

Contours are given in metres
The vertical interval is 5m

A24 Findon
3 km or 2 miles

Chanctonbury Ring, with its distinctive clump of storm-battered beech trees, is visible from miles around. A quarry cross-section shows how thin the downland soils are.

7 Washington to Amberley

past Chantry Post and Rackham Banks
6¼ miles (10.1 km)

From the South Downs Way car park at Washington to the A24 there are a number of fingerposts directing you to a point opposite Glazeby Lane. Crossing the A24 is tricky, the traffic is very fast and thunders by (see previous chapter for alternative safe crossing). Once across, there is a fingerpost: go north, parallel to the main road. Although once permitted, vehicles other than pedal cycles have now been prohibited from driving along the Way between Washington and Amberley, as the noise and disturbance spoilt the enjoyment of other users.

The lane has a verge wide enough for horses. After about 100 yards, it turns westwards and starts to climb a hill. There is a clearly marked water tap at this point. Opposite the entrance to Bostal Hill Farm there is another fingerpost pointing westwards up the steep tarmac path. Horses might find this section a little bit slippery in frosty weather as there is no verge. Pass another fingerpost as you leave the tarmac on to a flinty track. There is an ash hanger to the north through which you can see the Weald when the trees are leafless.

There is a strange metal and concrete bunker **44** almost at the top of the hill. It is an ugly building but an interesting piece of Britain's defensive history with gun ports pointing out over the Weald. Towards the top of Highden Hill, look back north-eastwards to Washington Church, with its square tower, and note the contrasting geology between the quarries of the Lower Greensand and the chalk pits. You can see Worthing and the sea to the south. A thick, low-lying mist may limit the views, but not being able to see the towns enhances the overall feeling of isolation. You can occasionally see smoke rising from a woodland fire down in the Weald, but the village of Storrington to the north-west, so distinct on the map (see page 103), is usually hidden by trees. To the south-east you get a clear but distant view of Cissbury Ring, even on hazy days.

The views from the top of Barnsfarm Hill (where the alternative route joins the Way) are primarily to the south, as you cannot see over the scarp slope. The track can be muddy here, but is level. The lines of the cross dyke, on the promontory of Sullington Hill, and trackway leading down to the scarp, are obvious.

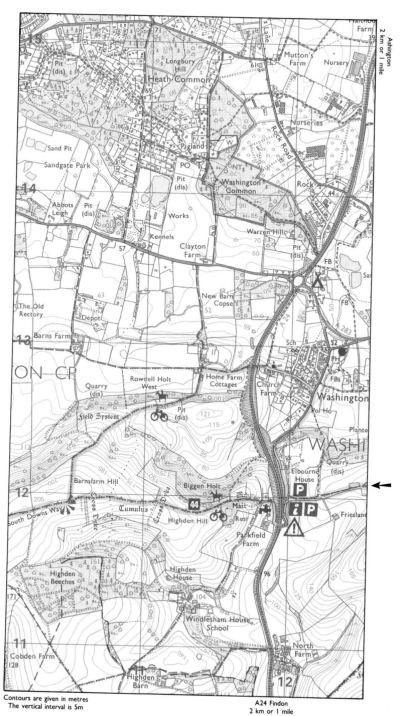

Contours are given in metres
The vertical interval is 5m

A24 Findon
2 km or I mile

From Steyning Bowl looking towards Cissbury Ring Iron Age fort.

To the north you can see the shrunken village of Sullington with a tiny Saxon church. In winter, it can be cool up here, so you have to walk at a brisk pace to keep warm.

At the southern end of the bridleway, coming up the eastern slope of Sullington Hill, there is a multiple path junction with a Dutch barn and two cattle troughs. At the barn you pass through a bridleway gate held closed by a crude chain. Beyond, the Way goes over a cattle grid, but there is a bridleway gate for riders. Occasional groups of walkers approach from the Chantry Post **45** cark park. This is a favourite kite-flying spot and can be a great joy for children.

Just before the car park, the Way goes over another cattle grid and horseriders will have to dismount to open a metal field gate. Chantry Post **45** is missing all its fingers, which is not much help! South is Harrow Hill with its enclosure marked on the top, and a superb line of trees to the west coming northwards from Lee Farm.

From the car park you pass through a number of arable fields with thorn trees on the boundaries. Just to the west, the path divides. Take the northernmost track, which is hard and chalky.

On grey days, shafts of sunlight pick out patches of the Downs, more rolling and wooded as you go westwards, with pink light on the sea to the south. From the top of Kithurst Hill the Way runs down to another car park at Springhead Hill, with

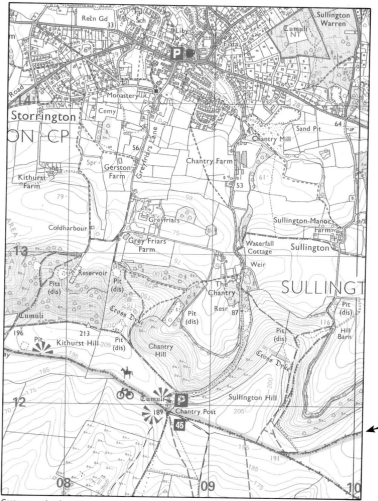

Contours are given in metres Lee Farm
The vertical interval is 5m

a fine clump of trees beyond. In this car park there is the white-painted Parham Post **46**, which is also missing two of its fingers. In addition there is an information board describing the Arun Valley Walks.

The Way climbs gently westwards to Springhead Hill, on compacted chalk that can be a bit 'greasy' in wet weather. As you approach the top, the track becomes very flinty, but it is broad enough for horses to ride on the softer verge. Sadly, the copse here was badly damaged in the 1987 storm, but it is still a fine landscape feature and there are already some lichens and fungi beginning to grow on the rotting timber. Take the northernmost bridleway running along the scarp slope. There is a South Downs Way fingerpost here, but it is set back a little behind some trees and easily missed. The cross dyke marked on the map seems to have been ploughed out, but about 160 yards (150 metres) west of the beech copse there are still the remains of a plundered tumulus, surrounded by small thorn trees.

The Way in winter – high on the Downs above Parham Park.

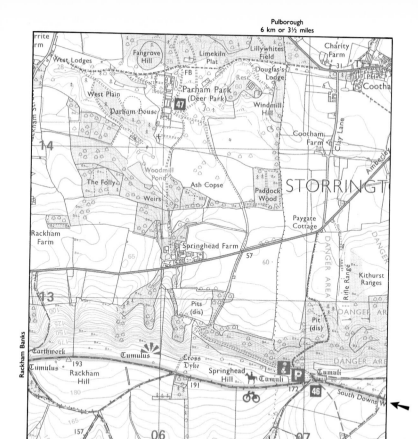

Contours are given in metres
The vertical interval is 5m

There are now fabulous views to the north over the Weald and Parham Deer Park **47**, with its house, woods, ponds and follies. The Way is now a rutted chalk track. The route is almost level, but gently climbs to Rackham Hill at 633 feet (193 metres). To the north you can see the River Arun winding through its water meadows.

Look out over Amberley Wild Brooks as you get towards Rackham Banks (see map on page 107). To the west lies Bury Hill and the Downs beyond, and on the valley floor to the north there is Rackham, with its little white and cream houses, and other villages in the distance.

The Way passes a trig point at Rackham Hill, but it is sometimes difficult to make out and may be almost invisible until you are upon it. From here, descend gently westwards towards Amberley and Houghton Bridge. About 180 yards (200

105

metres) west of the top of Rackham Hill you cross the substantial, but little understood earthwork, known as Rackham Banks **48**.

About 50 yards west of some more tumuli there is a stile and metal gate. Riders will probably have to dismount to open and shut it properly. The trail drops quite sharply through some good chalk grassland to Downs Farm, where there is a metal bridle gate with an iron field gate. This can be a muddy section of the route.

From Downs Farm you can just see the white face of Amberley chalk pits **49**, now an industrial museum. The route here is rather steep and stony, descending to a wooden bridle gate. The Way is particularly tricky after the gate and it might be best to lead a horse. At the bottom of this short, difficult section join a track where a fingerpost points you westwards along the curved, metalled road past a tile-hung house called 'Highdown'. You quickly come to another fingerpost directing you south-west down a little road called 'High Titten'. There are good views into the chalk pit **49**, the bottom of which is quite wooded. As you walk down High Titten, with a broad verge suitable for horses, there is a bank of trees covered in old man's beard sweeping round the chalk pit edge, and a seat for those who wish to stop and rest.

At the bottom of High Titten you meet the B2139 road. The Way goes south along the roadside with no pavements, so *great care* is required. Opposite the exit from the industrial museum there is a safe verge behind a low post-and-rail fence. The museum is well worth a visit. Access to it is gained via the Amberley railway station car park. There are regular services from this station and toilets on the platform (but they are sometimes padlocked).

Allow two hours to visit Amberley Chalk Pits Museum (open from April to October). It has a narrow-gauge quarry railway, a printer's shop, a blacksmith's shop, stationary engines, many other displays and a museum shop. The pub next to the railway station, the Bridge Inn, welcomes walkers and offers bed and breakfast, and food, both lunchtime and evenings. Nearby is a café, outside which is a drinking trough and water tap.

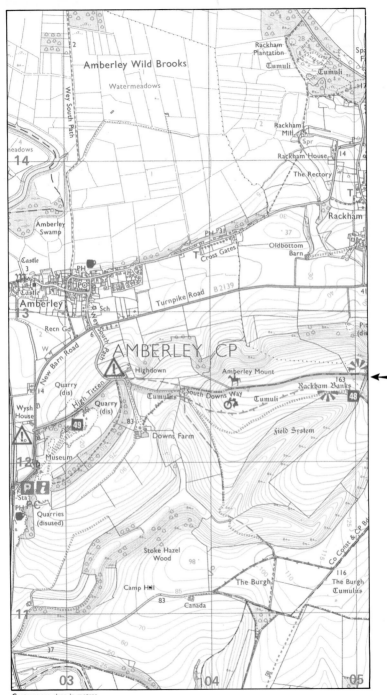

Contours are given in metres
The vertical interval is 5m

8 Amberley to Cocking

past Toby's Stone and Crown Tegleaze
11½ miles (18.5 km)

Leaving Amberley station, take great care as you head west over Houghton Bridge, where the Way runs on the roadside for half a mile (1 km) with no pavement. The tidal River Arun is enclosed by an embankment from which a number of little boat moorings jut into the water.

At the village of Houghton, the land rises above the flood-plain to the wooded slopes of the Downs. There is still no verge and it is rather dangerous walking. The parish church of St Nicholas is constructed of knapped flints – see how closely they are laid together. The quality of the farm buildings and workers' cottages indicates that this is a 'model' farm of one of the large estates.

At the T-junction in the centre of Houghton a fingerpost directs you north. The village pub lies 165 yards (150 metres) further west. The farmworkers' cottages are marked with the Duke of Norfolk's coronet and his letter 'N' monogram. One, just beyond the junction, has flakes of flint embedded in the mortar. This interesting technique is not common and is prob-ably both decorative and functional, in that the small flints reduce frost action. Many of the properties in the village are painted in the Duke's colours.

Go north now, past a timber-framed, thatched cottage. Look-ing back, eastwards over the water meadows, you can still see the white faces of Amberley chalk pits. After about 330 yards (300 metres) you come to a fingerpost and turn westwards again off the road.

The Way is a broad, flinty track passing through arable fields towards a clump of trees. Your route turns north-west and then west again as you rise. You pass a shepherd's caravan **50** on cast-iron wheels, like a little rusting shack. Towed to where lambing was taking place in winter, it provided a temporary home for the shepherd. Below, you can clearly see the meander-ing River Arun in the water meadows. In winter, Bury Church is visible to the north.

It is a steep climb, past Coombe Wood – a mixture of ash and beech with some holly on the fringes. There are huge fallen trees everywhere; their great, white, upended root plates all facing south.

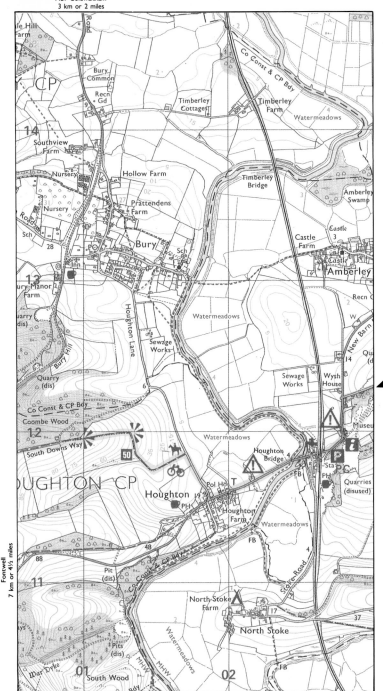

Contours are given in metres
The vertical interval is 5m

At the road junction a fingerpost points you north for about 100 yards. Cross to a wide verge on the other side. The Way westwards is signalled by another fingerpost and you leave the road towards Houghton Forest and Bury Hill.

The path levels off as you reach the top of the Downs where it meets a complex path junction **A**. Follow a fingerpost pointing you north-west. The Way rises gently towards Westburton Hill, and you can now see the radio masts between Sutton Down and Bignor Hill.

The huge expanse of Houghton Forest spreads out below to the south and west, giving a completely different character to the landscape. The Way becomes grassy – more comfortable underfoot for horses than the flinty track. You travel on the level, just off the scarp slope, along the contours. The only man-made feature visible is the isolated structure of King's Buildings to the west.

There are lots of skylarks and, in winter, flocks of fieldfares. The peace is disturbed only by the occasional plane passing overhead and by the faint 'popping' of shotguns. Your route comes gently off the back of Westburton Hill, heading north-westwards, and drops into a 'notch' in the Downs. There is a group of barns that sometimes houses overwintering cattle. Stop in the shelter or shade to have a snack before climbing Bignor Hill. The track can be very muddy from farm vehicle use. The wood to the west of the farm buildings has the wonderful name of Egg Bottom Coppice.

Just to the west there is a junction of paths. Follow the South Downs Way signposts south and then west again. The bridle-way leading down to Bignor and Bignor Roman Villa is sign-posted here. You wind steeply through scrubby woodland and, at the edge of the ash scrub, you find another fingerpost directing you through a bridle gate and then north-westwards. King's Buildings are just visible to the south of this turn, with Houghton Forest beyond. After about 80 yards (75 metres) the track curves westwards again towards the top of Bignor Hill.

Due north you can see the woodland and house of Bignor Park and to the east even the clump of Chanctonbury Ring is visible. At Toby's Stone **51**, the Way passes through a bridle gate: watch out for the cattle grid at dusk! The stone bears an inscription to James Wentworth Fitzwilliam Toby, once leader of the local hunt, and is in the form of a horse-mounting block. Much of the land to the west is owned by the National Trust and is open to the public. From Toby's Stone go west, climbing

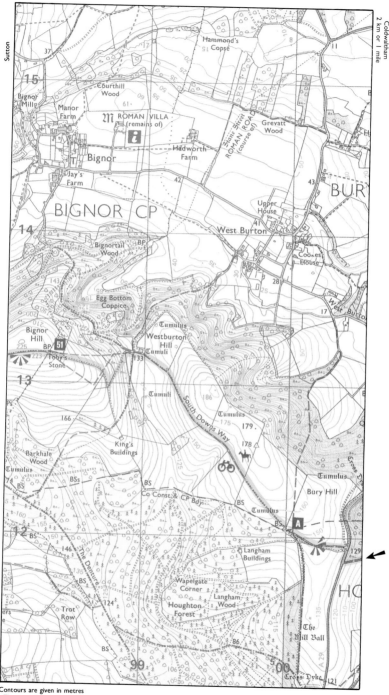

Sutton

Coldwaltham
2 km or 1 mile

Contours are given in metres
The vertical interval is 5m

quickly past the top of Bignor Hill and then dipping gently to the National Trust car park. As you descend there are beech woodlands blocking your view northwards. To the south lie the Neolithic camp of Barkhale **52** and the grassy mounds of tumuli. The track levels off just before you reach a cattle grid and bridle gate. Most people seem to skirt around the grid to the north.

The large 'Latin' signpost hints at the presence of a nearby Roman road, and beyond a clump of yews you come to the raised embankment or 'agger' of Stane Street **53**. Turn south-west on to this Roman road, which was constructed to connect the port of Chichester with London. Along it would have passed corn from the Downs, iron from the Weald and trade goods from the Continent. The views southwards from Stane Street looking towards the Roman farmlands of the coastal plain are spectacular. At a fingerpost, turn westwards off the Roman road.

A view from Gumber Farm along the raised 'agger' of Stane Street.

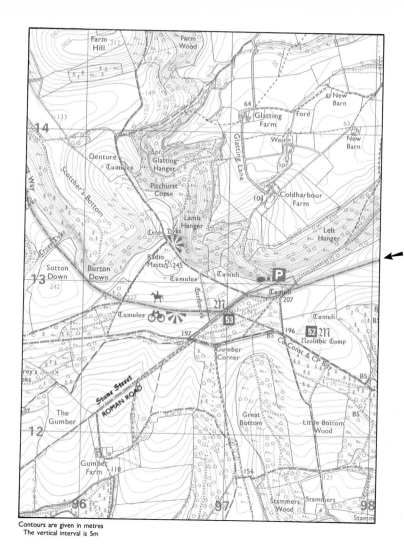

Contours are given in metres
The vertical interval is 5m

The trail is now a broad farm track with scrub to the south and arable fields to the north and the two radio masts dominating the landscape. You hardly notice the earthworks marked on the map. To the south-west you can see Chichester Cathedral and the sea beyond. On the western side of the field, at a multiple bridleway junction, a signpost points you north-westwards. You follow the edge of the beech, ash and yew woodland of Burton Down. The Way cuts across a pronounced Cross Dyke above Scotcher's Bottom, where there is a field gate. Descend gently along a broad, sometimes muddy track from Sutton

113

Down towards Littleton Farm and the A285. At the next cross dyke, pass through a rickety bridle gate.

To the north-west the battered clump of Bishop's Ring **54** stands out above the woodland of Woolavington Down. Notice the variety of trees alongside your route as the Way begins to drop steeply towards the main road. This is a dry, chalky track in summer, but in winter becomes a slippery mire. Thankfully a little raised walkway has been constructed near the farm.

At the road junction you go north about 20 yards before turning north-west again at a signpost. The Way skirts Littleton

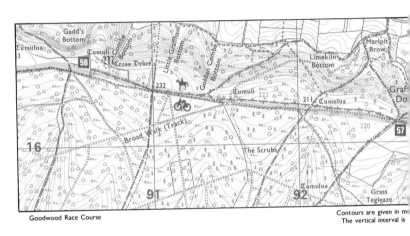

Goodwood Race Course

Contours are given in me
The vertical interval is

Farm past a number of farm entrances and through a bridle gate. Climb steeply up to Littleton Down. This hillside is one of the few places where the South Downs Way is regularly ploughed, so be prepared for some rough going. After passing through another bridle gate, the Way levels off and continues north-westwards to a group of woods. Nearby is Crown Tegleaze **55**, at 830 feet (253 metres) the highest point on the Downs. As you continue, you will find ash coppice, beech, yew and conifers.

After about 330 yards (300 metres) you leave the woodland and come to a multiple junction with a weathered signpost **56** erected by the Cowdrey Hunt. The views to the north and west are stunning. Continue to the cross dyke where a number of paths meet and just before a second dyke you cross a byway. The route runs on the farm tracks to the north of the tree belt. At Graffham Down there is an oak fingerpost **57** erected by the Society of Sussex Downsmen to commemorate one of their more dynamic members, Sir Edmond Barkworth.

The Way enters the dark woodland and the lack of direct sunshine makes this a very muddy section. A large clearing along Graffham Down is managed by the Graffham Trust to protect chalk grassland plants and butterflies.

As you come close to a forestry track called Broad Walk a signpost indicates the Way ahead and a kink in the route. Head towards a series of cross dykes. Heyshott Down archaeological site **58**, managed by the Society of Sussex Downsmen, contains a group of Bronze Age burial mounds dating from about 1500 BC, which mark the sites of cremations placed in pottery vessels.

The Way curves briefly southwards and then again westwards. Your route now is through arable fields just off the top of the scarp slope along the northern edge of the woodland.

Contours are given in metres
vertical interval is 5m

Halnaker
7 km or 4½ miles

115

The shadows cast by the sun highlight the terracettes on the steep scarp slopes of the Downs.

Pass south of a trig point standing in the middle of a large field. To the west you can see what appears to be a forestry lookout tower, in fact a raised platform for shooting deer. You will notice a few of these peculiar contraptions gently rotting away. They were constructed by the Cowdrey Estate as a money-making venture. Thankfully, it seems to have failed! Near the shooting tower on top of the small reservoir there are views westwards towards Cocking Down and north to the Weald.

At the most westerly cross dyke **59** on Heyshott Down the Way kinks and passes by a field gate through this prominent dyke. From this point the track dries out as you descend towards Cocking Hill – a fast downhill run for mountain bikers. At Manorfarm Down the Way parts company with the woodland.

To the south of Hill Barn there is a huge timber yard full of seasoning wood, and cottages whose bright yellow paintwork indicates that they belong to the Cowdrey Estate. One is tile-hung with Upper Greensand walls. This is an unusual material to see on the Downs, but is the local stone in the scarp-foot villages. Nearby is a tap for South Downs Way travellers, but the water is turned off in winter.

Continue down Hillbarn Lane to the A286 where there is a small car park. If you wish to visit the fascinating collection of reconstructed medieval Weald and Downland buildings, turn south 2½ miles (3.9 km) to Singleton.

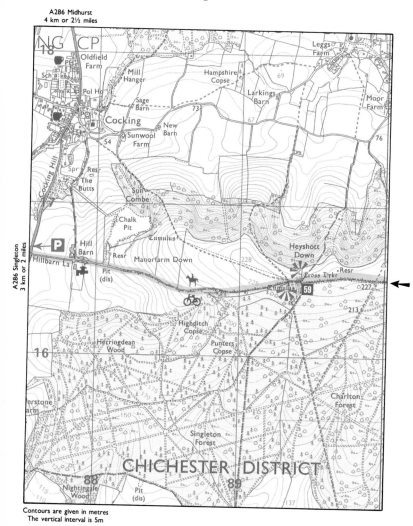

Contours are given in metres
The vertical interval is 5m

Cowdrey Park, off the Way at Midhurst, was built around 1530 and destroyed

in 1793.

A circular walk on Slindon Estate

2½ miles (3.9 km)

This walk starts at Bignor Hill car park and has been laid out by the National Trust, who have owned and managed the area since the 1950s.

The route is marked with white waymarking and takes you south-west down Stane Street **53**, and beyond the route of the South Downs Way, to the highest point on Stane Street (646 feet/197 metres). This was probably used by the Romans as a major survey point. The raised 'agger' on the Roman road was reserved for official messengers and army manoeuvres; other people used the lower 'slow lane'.

The land marked as The Gumber on the map was once a rabbit warren. During the Second World War it was a 'dummy' airfield to deflect bombing raids from the real base at Tangmere.

Continue down the Roman road for about 50 yards and then turn south at the viewpoint. Work your way back to Gumber Corner, following the path. The woods that you pass are another example of the damage caused by the storm of 1987. The National Trust aims to leave the majority of the wind-blown

The footpath running beside Stane Street, near Bignor Hill.

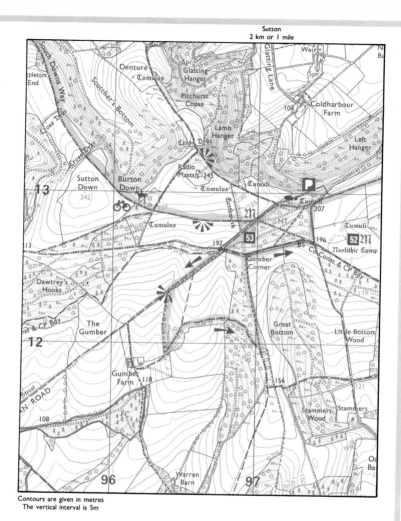

Contours are given in metres
The vertical interval is 5m

trees to act as a food source for wood-eating insects and the other wildlife that lives on them. Eventually new trees will recolonise the area. To the north, a plantation of beech has Scots pine acting as a 'nurse' against the wind. The pines will be thinned out, leaving a mature beech woodland.

From Gumber Corner return to the car park, or make a brief detour to Barkhale Neolithic camp **52**. This has been plough-damaged in the past and is one of the largest causewayed enclosures ever discovered. It has 13 separate entrances and was probably used as a tribal meeting place, where stock was slaughtered for the winter and religious and social festivals were held.

9 Cocking to Buriton

passing the Devil's Jumps and Harting Hill
11 miles (17.9 km)

From the car park on the A286, head westwards up Middlefield Lane. Once through Cockinghill Farm the path climbs gently towards Cocking Down between machine-trimmed hedgerows, and becomes a sunken track cut deeply into the chalk by years of use. Continue past a couple of farm tracks, and as you gain height the hedges disappear.

To the south you can see the grandstand of Goodwood racecourse and the two radio masts of the Trundle. The Way runs level along the top of the Downs. The views are primarily to the south-west over the woodlands. There are arable fields either side, with no view to the north, as you are just off the scarp slope.

Just before reaching the ploughed-out cross dyke you can see the spire of Chichester Cathedral to the south-east. Beyond the dyke, there is a small line of beech trees alongside a bridleway,

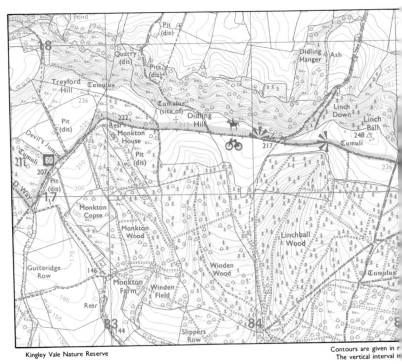

Kingley Vale Nature Reserve

Contours are given in r
The vertical interval is

leading south to Kingley Vale Nature Reserve, famous for its ancient yew woodland. You pass a crude, wooden ladder leading to a deer-shooting platform.

The landscape here is plateau-like and the Way descends very gently from Linch Ball to Treyford Hill. There are mole hills on the verges, but even these are full of chalk rubble, which shows how shallow the soil is here. The woodland of Didling Hanger reaches right up to the South Downs Way. Just beyond, there are good views to the north. The trail becomes a grassy track, enclosed by sheep fences.

West of Didling Hill the route enters woodland above Monkton House and the Way can be very muddy because of over-shading. It curves to the south-west, passing a bracken glade. Oddly, the highest fire risk period is in winter, when the fronds are dry. About 100 yards south-west of a signpost, you can see the grassy mounds of the Devil's Jumps tumuli **60**. For a closer view, leave the route by a little path. This is a spectacular group of large tumuli.

About 550 yards (500 metres) south-west of the Devil's Jumps **60**, turn north-westwards along a broad track through the

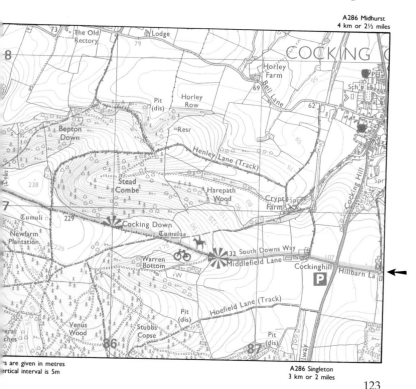

woodland, where new trees have been planted in plastic tubes, looking like a military cemetery. You pass a tiny memorial **61** to Hauptman Joseph Oesterman – a German pilot killed during the Second World War?

At the high point in Philliswood Down you can see westwards to Telegraph House **62**, which commemorates the sending of semaphore messages via this hill during the Napoleonic Wars. To the north and west you can see the features of Pen Hill and Beacon Hill beyond Buriton Farm.

You descend a broad chalky track to a 'kink' in the Way above Buriton Farm and pass through your first bridle gate of the day. From here go north-westwards between barbed-wire fences on a well-trodden grassy track. There is an open feeling here with some views to the north over the Weald. The trail just touches the woodland above Rook Clift. This is a narrow, and occasionally rather muddy, section as you wind around the head of a valley.

Go round the headland above Elsted Hanger. At Mount Sinai, about 100 yards beyond a byway crossing, a fingerpost directs you westwards to Pen Hill up a steep, broad track, a little distance from the woodland. As you rise there are fine views, particularly eastwards along the scarp slope. This is a good riding surface, softer than some of the other tracks. The Way then curves down to a cross dyke. Beyond this the Way rises gently and curves southwards, towards Telegraph House **62**, taking a less steep route around Beacon Hill. Although less difficult than going directly west, it is still quite a climb at first.

Continue south along the contours of Beacon Hill, and just touch the outer ramparts of its Iron Age fort **63**. About 30 yards into some woodland you come to a South Downs Way fingerpost directing you north-west.

In winter you will see the beautiful orange-red berries of climbing bryony among the thorn trees. As you head back around the west side of Beacon Hill you might put up a small flock of feral pigeons from the stubble. To the south-west you can usually just make out the water of Chichester Harbour.

Drop gently into Bramshott Bottom. At the head of this dry valley, the Way suddenly turns west again and there are two fingerposts here. Climb steeply through the scrub to the top of Harting Downs. There are clearly two parallel paths here, both well used. You can now see the green copper spire of South Harting Church **64** (see map on page 127) in the village at the foot of the Downs. Westwards there is a radio mast on top of

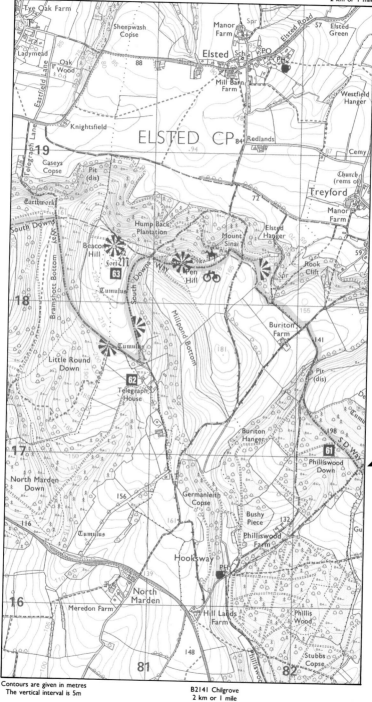

Contours are given in metres
The vertical interval is 5m

B2141 Chilgrove
2 km or 1 mile

Butser Hill. The cross dykes, where the track coming up from Whitcombe Bottom meets the Way, are visible.

Looking west from a small clump of cankered ash, you can see the car park at Harting Hill and the ruined folly **65** of Tower Hill, surrounded by trees. Descend gently down a broad, flinty track and through a wooden bridle gate. There is a busy road, the B2141, coming up the scarp. On the far side go north-west on a narrow, sandy track, through woodland.

The Way levels out to meet the B2146. To the south lies Up Park (commonly spelt Uppark), a 1690s country house owned by the National Trust and sadly damaged by fire in 1989. After crossing the road, you go westwards along a broad, flinty farm track called 'Forty Acre Lane'. From here it is a 2-mile (3-km), almost level, and sometimes very muddy, run to the West Sussex–Hampshire boundary at Hundred Acres. The views are primarily to the north to Torberry Hill **66** and South Harting. The most dominant landscape feature is the forestry plantation

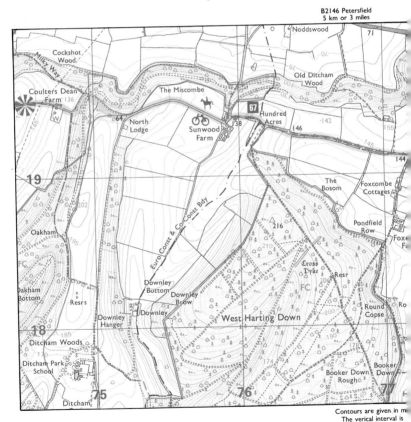

of West Harting Down. You cross the Sussex Border Path just north of Foxcombe Farm.

From the top of the hill at Hundred Acres descend gently towards Sunwood Farm. The unmarked county boundary **67** was the official end of the South Downs Way until it was extended to Winchester in 1989. Go south, then west through the farm. The trail rises towards The Miscombe on a metalled road beside a line of beech trees.

Just before North Lodge the road turns south towards Ditcham Park School. Take a fork going westwards towards Coulters Dean Farm. The Hampshire section of the Way is not clearly waymarked. Your route goes steeply down through the woods. At a sharp bend there is a sign saying 'Cart Track Buriton' (marked on the map as 'Milky Way'). Here you curve south-west, then west to Coulters Dean Farm. Leave the tarmac and pass beneath a power line. To your south you can see the woodland of Oakham and to the north good views over the

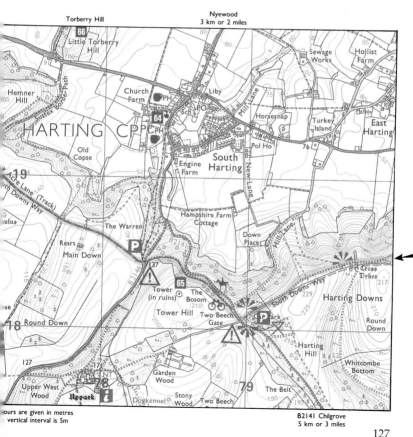

Weald. At the high point above Coulters Dean Farm, you can see a quarry at Fagg's Farm, the woodland of Ludgersham Copse and Head Down Plantation ahead to the west.

The Way undulates towards Dean Barn and can be very sticky and slippery in wet weather. You go through the woodland of Appleton's Copse and descend steeply to Newbarn Road, along a sunken lane lined with hazel, ash and old man's beard. Opposite is parking for Queen Elizabeth Country Park **68**. From here you can go down Kiln Lane into Buriton.

Queen Elizabeth Country Park is renowned for its ancient farm **69** (see also page 130), which is open from April to September and worth a visit. You can also see various displays on forestry and sheep management in the Park Centre.

The ancient farm has reconstructed Iron Age houses, rare animals, plants and a herb garden, as well as demonstrations of pottery-making and metallurgy.

The 'blues' – a rather special group of butterflies

As you walk the Way you should spot some of the butterflies from the 'blue' family. These include the adonis, chalk hill, small, common, and holly blues, while oddly enough the brown argus is also included in the group. Two (the chalk hill and adonis) are particularly characteristic downland insects, which need the food plant horseshoe vetch and short, sheep-grazed turf.

Surprisingly they have developed a mutually beneficial relationship with the yellow meadow ant. The butterfly larvae and pupae are protected by the ants. In return they produce a honey-like secretion which the ants love. A case of Darwinian 'you scratch my back and I'll scratch yours!'

The hot south-facing slopes of the Downs are one of the few habitats in Britain warm enough to support the adonis blue, while you are more likely to see the holly blue on wooded downland in West Sussex. It is a real joy to discover these subtle, unpretentious, but superbly beautiful insects as you journey between Eastbourne and Winchester.

Bopeep
Copse
108
Copyhold
Barn
New
Barn
Bolinge Hill
Farm
Hoadlands
Crundle
88
Black Hill
Cottages
21
82
Whiteland
Copse
83
Sewage
Works
Quarry
(disused)
Glebe
Farm
PH
Buriton
House
Queen Elizabeth
Country Park
Sch
Buriton
20
Quarry
(disused)
POs
South La
Tumulus
FB
Woolmer
Pond
Buriton
Hanger
Tumuli
Pit
(dis)
Appleton's
Copse
Tumuli
Fagg's
Farm
144
Resr
BURITON CP
Dean
Barn
Tunnel
War Down
205
Ludgersham
Copse
19
Queen Elizabeth
Country Park
Newbarn Road
Head Down
Plantation
191
FC
Wolver
Row
68
Gravelhill
Bottom
Benhams
Bushes
204
Gorecombe
Hole
FC
195
FC
Queen Elizabeth Forest
Holt Down
Plantation
New
Barn
Head Down
Hanger
140
18
137
Newbarn
Hanger
125
ROMAN
BUILDING
(site of)
137
Settlement
(site of)
Glass Brow
148
Chalton Park
72
Chalton
Down
135
73
74

A3(T) Horndean
7 km or 4½ miles

Contours are given in metres
The vertical interval is 5m

129

10 Buriton to Exton

via Butser Hill and Old Winchester Hill
12¼ miles (19.6 km)

The route from here to Winchester will eventually be a continuous bridleway, but some sections have still to be confirmed. Although the entire highlighted route is open to walkers, riders sometimes have to use alternatives. Waymarks will indicate future changes in proposed route alignment or status.

From the western end of the Queen Elizabeth Country Park car park near Buriton, go through a bridle gate and follow a broad, gravel track rising and curving south-westwards. The path levels off overlooking Fagg's Farm.

Just past a post, painted red with a white horseshoe, you come to a fork in the track. The country park riding trail lies straight ahead, but the Way drops to the south-west down Gravelhill Bottom. Descend gently through the woodland to a clearing, equipped for picnics and barbecues. Horseriders should follow one of the many permissive routes. After a mile (1.5 km) there is another clearing called Benhams Bushes. Where the metalled forest road forms a huge arc there is another car park and picnic site. The trail goes south-west across a grassy track, and downhill, taking the lower of the two roads.

At the bottom of the hill there are lots of signs relating to the country park **68** (see page 128) and numerous tracks leading off the internal park road – it is all very confusing. There is a horse-box park here. Head north for about 275 yards (250 metres) to the Park Centre. Horses are not welcome at the Centre, so the bridleway passes just east in the woodland. There is a café, toilets, ice-cream vendor and a large shop here.

On leaving the Centre, go east to the rear of the building and you will see a green sign indicating Butser Hill Iron Age farm **69** (see page 128). Head north, pass under the main road, and rejoin the park bridleway. After about 30 yards you come to the end of a wooden railing and cross the tarmac to the farm.

Northwards, away from the farm, follow the bridleway signs. You can see the climb ahead. Drop to a bridle gate, past public toilets (open in summer) and a small weather station.

The Way continues under an electricity line. The pasture is ideal for horses, but very steep. You pass through a Bronze/Iron Age field system. About half a mile (750 metres) up Butser Hill go through a bridle gate with a stile next to it.

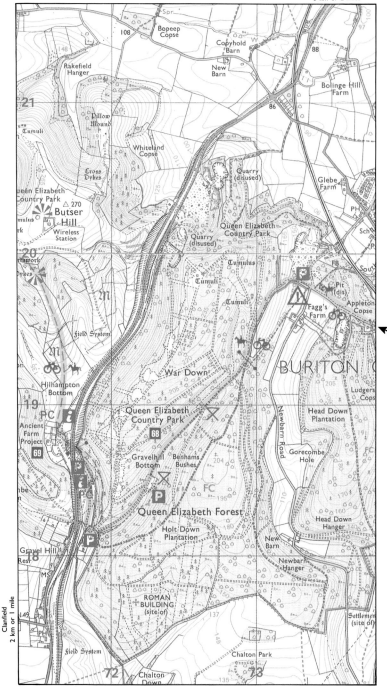

Contours are given in metres
The vertical interval is 5m

The whole of this hillside is used extensively for sports such as hang gliding, grass skiing and model-aircraft flying, and can be a colourful, busy place. By contrast, it is also an excellent spot for downland flowers and insects. Go west of the radio masts through another narrow bridle gate. There is a board across the bottom which is easy to trip over, so take care. Curve around in a great arc and head towards Limekiln Lane. The number of cross dykes and Bronze Age tumuli suggest that this was a strategic site. It is worth deviating to the trig point, near the masts, from where you can get panoramic views northwards.

Near the top of Butser Hill a mock Iron Age roundhouse forms a café, toilets and information centre. The café is closed in the winter, but there is a car park, picnic site, emergency telephone and water point.

The Way passes through a narrow, brambly section just before it hits Limekiln Lane and leaves the country park. The route runs parallel to the road on the verge-side, but about 100 yards from the car park you are forced by barbed-wire fencing on to the highway for about half a mile (1 km).

Butser Hill is the end of the dramatic section of the South Downs, and westwards the chalk forms a rolling plateau. Looking east, you can see the fire breaks of Queen Elizabeth Forest running straight up and down the hillside. To the west are two radio masts on Wether Down near the naval base of HMS *Mercury*. You come to a multiple road junction and the Way turns due west along a lane marked 'unsuitable for motors'

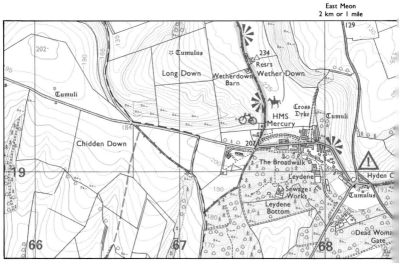

East Meon
2 km or 1 mile

Contours are given in m
The vertical interval is

towards Tegdown Hill. You now have about 1¼ miles (2 km) of almost level journey to Hyden Cross.

Past a clump of six monkey-puzzle trees next to Homelands Farm the road deteriorates into a grass track and there are high hedges of laurel, holly, beech and thorn. Continue westwards under the electricity line, with expansive views to the north. At low points on Tegdown Hill, the Way can be muddy and wet.

From this ridge you can see the church at East Meon and the river valley below you. The grassy ruts just to the north show that this has been a thoroughfare for many centuries. As you enter Hyden Wood, it feels like a pretty woodland walk, but a few trees have fallen across the Way and the going can be very wet. When you descend towards HMS *Mercury* the track gets a little drier, and there is a sheltered spot in which to sit and eat your lunch.

The Way goes past a black and white thatched cottage up the Droxford road to a junction about 100 yards ahead. Riders and pedestrians should take care. Go straight across the second junction down Hyden Farm Lane. Pass the main entrance to HMS *Mercury* and head briefly in a north-westerly direction. After about 100 yards the road curves sharply around to head westwards again through HMS *Mercury*. At the western end the road meets another junction. Go north on to a gravelly track that rises gently towards the high point at Wether Down. You are suddenly back in open rolling downland with superb views in most directions.

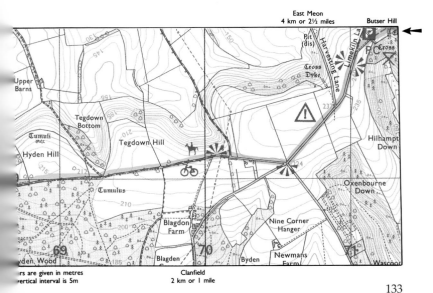

133

Beyond Wetherdown Barn, towards Salt Hill, the trail can be very muddy and slippery. The Way drops steeply off Salt Hill to the small hamlet of Coombe Cross. The trees are low here, so riders should be careful. Down the slope the lane becomes a hard, sunken track. About 550 yards (500 metres) south of Coombe Cross the Way levels out and is a quagmire in winter. Continue northwards, across the metalled road, and back on to the byway.

About 275 yards (250 metres) north of Coombe Cross the track kinks. It is dry even though enclosed by trees. The Way descends gently towards Henwood Down. At a dip you reach a signpost and turn westwards on the bridleway through a metal field gate along a grassy headland. Mountain bikers coming down from Coombe Cross should be careful of deep potholes as they approach this turning.

Head west as the ground rises over the slopes of Henwood Down, with Hen Wood to the north. To the south you can see

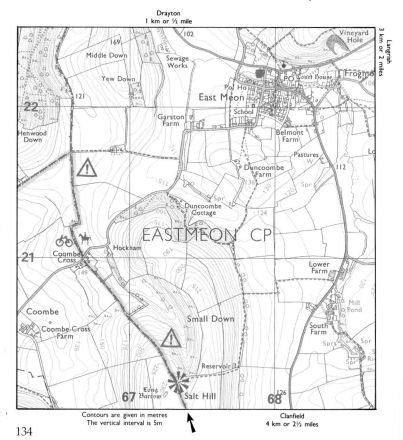

The South Downs Way near the hamlet of Coombe Cross looking towards Hen Wood.

the radio masts close to HMS *Mercury*. Whitewool Farm **70** and Whitewool Hanger lie to the west below Old Winchester Hill **71**. Pass through another metal field gate where the bridleway becomes a concrete farm track.

On reaching the minor road, turn north-westwards by Hall Cottages. Follow the signpost to Whitewool Farm **70** past the 'No entry cattle only' driveway and the asbestos barn with the big, galvanized feed hoppers. Turn south-west at a sign saying 'to the farm' and carry on down the track. North-west is Whitewool Pond with a brick dam at its northern end. The driveway curves around the main farm, goes southwards briefly and then, after passing through a metal gate, turns west towards Old Winchester Hill **71**. There is a disused chalk pit ahead of you cut into the hillside below a beech hanger.

At the pit, take the route north-westwards through a heavy metal gate, diagonally up the hill towards the road. The Countryside Commission's proposed route cuts westwards up to the northern end of the woodland, but it is not yet open, so continue to the road at the top of the hill.

You come to another metal gate and a fingerpost. On reaching the woodland along the roadside, the verge disappears and there is a warning sign.

Parking here gives access to Old Winchester Hill **71**, a popular national nature reserve. The proposed route passes to the east, parallel to the road, through the woodland, but as this section of the path is not open, you should go through the gaps into the reserve. Old Winchester Hill is surmounted by an Iron Age fort **72**, whose defensive earthworks, probably from the 2nd century BC, may have been a tribal centre for the region east of the Meon River. The reserve is maintained by sheep grazing, so keep your dog on a lead. Follow the nature trail around the hill. Horse-riders and cyclists may eventually be able to enter the reserve through a bridle gate opposite the southern end of the roadside wood. At the point where the main reserve access track meets the nature trail there is an interpretative board. About 50 yards west you come to a fork and a white-painted post with a black arrow. The South Downs Way winds around the southern edge of the reserve and the nature trail follows the arrows to the information centre. Overall it is level walking, but can be muddy in winter due to heavy pedestrian use. As the main track curves westwards you see the spectacular ramparts of the Iron Age fort **72** ahead. Here there is a stile and a kissing gate next to a locked field gate.

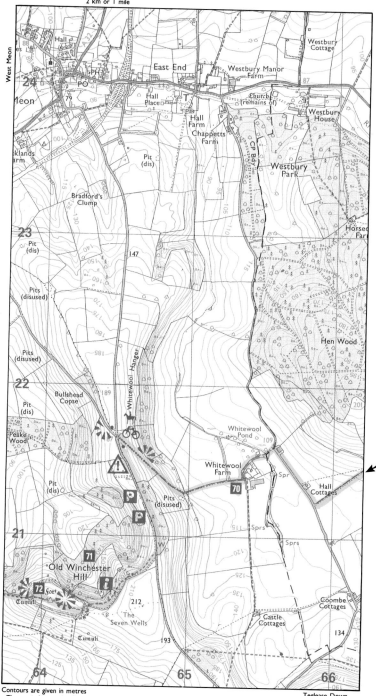

West Meon

Meon

West Meon

Hall

PH

PO

24

79

08

klands arm

Bradford's Clump

23

Pit (dis)

147

Pits (disused)

Pits (disused)

22

Bullshead Copse

Pit (dis)

Peake Wood

Pit (dis)

21

71

Old Winchester Hill

72 Fort

Tumuli

The Seven Wells

212

Tumuli

193

64

65

66

East End

Hall Place

Hall Farm

Chappetts Farm

Westbury Manor Farm

Church (remains of)

Westbury Cottage

Westbury House

Westbury Park

Horsed Far

Hen Wood

201

Whitewool Hanger

Whitewool Pond 109

Whitewool Farm

70

Spr

Hall Cottages

115

Sprs

Sprs

120

125

135

140

Coombe Cottages

134

Castle Cottages

Pits (disused)

CP Bdy

It is proposed that the bridleway section will turn south and run around the outer edge of the earthworks in the adjoining field. Pedestrians, after travelling 50 yards south, can turn west again and walk directly across the Iron Age fort. Next to the trig point, there is a panoramic viewfinder. On a clear day you can see the Isle of Wight and Chichester Harbour.

The path now drops steeply to a gate and stile and into a small woodland, mostly of yew and ash. At the edge of the trees you come to another gate and a wooden fingerpost. Then, after the end of a sheep fence, you come to a waymark signalling the route north to Roll's Copse **73** along a headland on the western side of another fence.

Where the Way kinks west and then north you take the higher farm track above woodland, past a huge hole on the high track, caused by badgers digging their sett. At Roll's Copse **73** the Way briefly meets a concrete road and then turns westwards through a farm gate on to a gravelly path towards Exton. Before reaching the disused railway line the trail becomes a deeper, sunken track, which in winter can be very wet, as you are following the

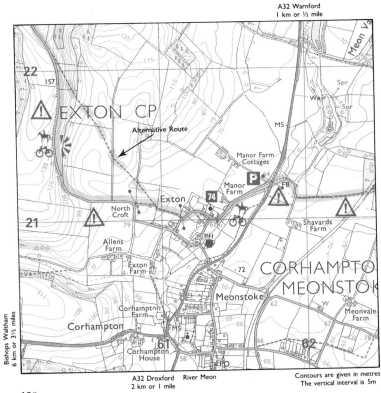

138

bed of a winter-flowing chalk stream. Many walkers take the higher route on the bank alongside. The path is blocked for horses by low overhanging trees and a couple of large, fallen ash branches that you have to skirt. It is just passable for pedestrians and cyclists.

The Way passes under the disused railway line through a brick arch. About 200 yards to the west a series of sharp angle irons driven into the bed of the stream would be dangerous to riders. After a single-sleeper bridge, the Way turns northwards. The path can be very muddy as you approach the River Meon. This is a beautiful chalk stream with a footbridge wide enough for pedestrians and cyclists. Horses can ford the river just to the south. Turn south-west to reach the main road and cross with care to the low-lying country lane opposite. The Way curves westwards through Exton, going north of the pub and just south of the church **74**. Inside the church, a remarkable head-stone shows the angel of death summoning the scholar from his books. After a 12-mile (19-km) walk through the winter mud, you may feel as if he's summoning you as well!

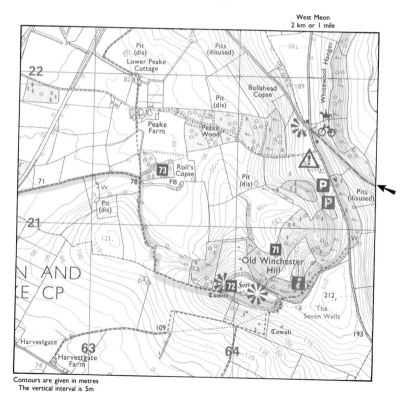

Contours are given in metres
The vertical interval is 5m

11 Exton to Winchester

through Lomer and Chilcomb
12 miles (19.5 km)

The Way goes westwards, past Exton Church **74**, along the curved main street with a high brick and then flint wall on your south side. At a bridleway sign you turn north-west between Glebe Cottage and Bramcote House.

The Way is a grassy track for 50 yards before it passes through a metal gate next to a stile and runs along a field headland. After about 100 yards the Way turns north through a gap and then turns west again on the other side of the fence. At the kink you pass a footpath junction, where you could head north-west avoiding the road section, but there is no signpost. Just past a bungalow, go through a metal field gate and rejoin the road. On this climb to Beacon Hill **75**, it is proposed to establish a bridleway in the field alongside. There is little or no verge, so take care.

The River Meon, crossed by this bridge north of Exton, is an attractive chalk stream.

Bishops Waltham
6 km or 3½ miles

Contours are given in metres
The vertical interval is 5m

Droxford
2 km or 1 mile

   As you rise, the route is cut into the hillside, with old man's beard, and ivy-covered ash trees forming a great arch for the sun to filter through. It is a lovely, cool place in summer with lots of small birds singing. Suddenly, about halfway up the hill, a magnificent view opens over the Meon Valley. As you gain height, the ash trees become stunted, and you get glimpses of Beacon Hill **75** to the north, with its nature reserve of buff-coloured chalk grassland.

   The Way curves north-westwards as you approach the top of the hill. Just as you level off, there is a fingerpost and a stile, next to an iron field gate, indicating the safe footpath route back to Exton. A hundred yards north-west there is a proposal that you turn north and head to Beacon Hill and Beaconhill Beeches. This

141

is not yet possible, so carry on up the road. At the highest point there is a gap in the hedge with a stile and fingerpost. Pedestrians can cut off the zigzag roadside section here. At the first junction you continue north-west. After about 100 yards, at a T-junction, turn sharply north-east, then north-west again after a further 150 yards. At this point there is a suitable site for unboxing horses. After about 275 yards (250 metres) the road turns north and you carry on ahead, along a footpath.

Even in January, this broad, dry, flinty track provides a comfortable route for walkers and cyclists, but may be a little hard for horses.

Trees line the path as you approach Lomer Pond, with a mixture of oak, ash and beech and an understorey of blackthorn and holly. Just north-west of Lomer Cottage, there are humps and bumps in the field – all that remains of a lost, medieval village **76**.

As you approach Lomer the Way levels and is more enclosed by hedges and trees. Turn south-west for about 50 yards, then curve westwards, within the farmyard, south of two farm cottages. Past the second cottage you turn north for about 30 yards and then west again along a broad farm track. There is a small oak post here with a white-painted top and a black waymark arrow, indicating that the Wayfarer's Walk, from Emsworth in Hampshire to Inkpen Beacon near Newbury, has now joined the South Downs Way.

The trail winds westwards for half a mile (1 km) through a mixed arable and woodland landscape. The route is frequently used by farm vehicles and can be rather wet underfoot, but as the ground rises the going improves and becomes grassy. You can often hear the raucous call of cock pheasants in this vicinity, and there is spiky green witches'-broom to be seen in the hedgeline.

As you approach the road there are views over rolling downland to the north-east. You can see Hinton Ampner House in The Park near New Cheriton, and Cheriton to the north. Wind Farm **77**, with a notice for travellers saying 'This is Wind Farm', is an early Victorian flint-and-brick cottage, constructed with a mixture of tiles, slate and patterned bricks.

Follow the track and turn north through a beech copse to join the road. Cross carefully. On the opposite side a fingerpost indicates the Wayfarers Walk going north-east. Turn west along the verge, then there is about 1¼ miles (2 km) of roadside walking. Remember to face oncoming traffic. Just before a

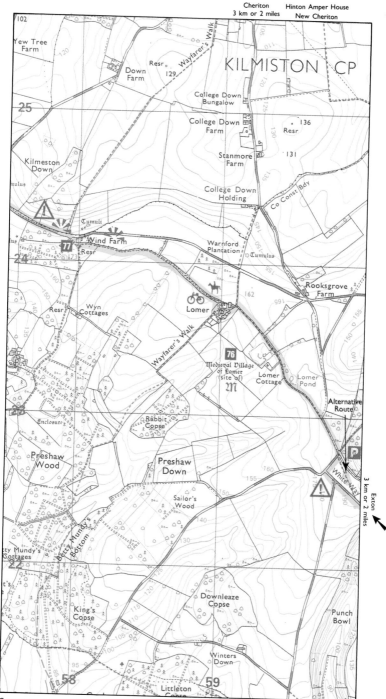

KILMISTON CP

Yew Tree Farm

Down Farm

Resr
129

Wayfarer's Walk

College Down Bungalow

College Down Farm

25

136
Resr

Kilmiston Down

131

Stanmore Farm

130

College Down Holding

Co Const Bdy

Tumuli

77

Wind Farm

Resr

Warnford Plantation

Tumulus

24

162

Rooksgrove Farm

991

Wyn Cottages

Resr

Lomer

Wayfarer's Walk

76

Medieval Village of Lomer (site of)

Lomer Cottage

Lomer Pond

Enclosure

Preshaw Wood

Rabbit Copse

Preshaw Down

Alternative Route

P

White Way

Sailor's Wood

3 km or 2 miles

Exton

Betty Mundy's Bottom

ty Mundy's Cottages

22

Downleaze Copse

King's Copse

Punch Bowl

58

59

Winters Down

Littleton Copse

Contours are given in metres
The vertical interval is 5m

143

T-junction signposted Kilmeston, by the entrance to Preshaw House, the views northwards are beautiful.

Adjacent to the road junction is 'Mill Barrows' **78** – a distinct grassy knoll. It is an ancient burial mound and the local hill top, Millbarrow Down, is named after it. About 330 yards (300 metres) west you come to a crossroads where you turn north.

The pub shown as the 'Fox and Hounds' on the map has been renamed 'Milburys'. There is a treadmill inside that used to draw water from a deep well cut in the chalk. The barmaid will tell you all sorts of fables and give you ice cubes to drop down the well. From Milburys, go north about 100 yards and then turn north-west towards High Greendowns (now called High Stoke). From here, the Way descends north-westwards towards Holding Lane. Where the tarmac road turns north-east, continue in a northerly direction, past a Dutch barn. Holding Lane can be a little muddy in places, but is usually a level, dry, farm track.

The path drops gently towards Ball's Lane and your route beyond is a broad farm track lined with beech trees among arable fields. You see the cottages on the A272 beyond Holding Farm before catching glimpses of the agricultural buildings that lie in a little dip. The iron field gates here are generally left open. Note the neat system to enable riders to open the gate catch. Amazing what farmers can do with baler twine!

Go through a double wooden field gate by the road, cross with great care, and carry on in a northerly direction, rising gently past the cottages. After about 275 yards (250 metres) you come to another farm gate. Go through the gate and along the headland. At the easternmost corner of the field you come to a cattle trough and then a metal field gate where you do a U-turn and head north-west along the fence-line. There is a proposal to make a more direct route here. North-east of Ganderdown Farm the South Downs Way becomes a sunken track. Pass through a set of double field gates, for which horseriders will have to dismount.

Under the electricity lines go through a wooden bridle gate alongside a field gate. The Way is bounded by two neatly cut hedges and rises gently north-westwards towards a Dutch barn on the skyline. On top of Gander Down a bridleway leads north-east to Cheriton. Looking back to Ganderdown Farm, there seems to be a Celtic or medieval field system in the pasture land. There are extensive views to the north and the landscape is still plateau-like.

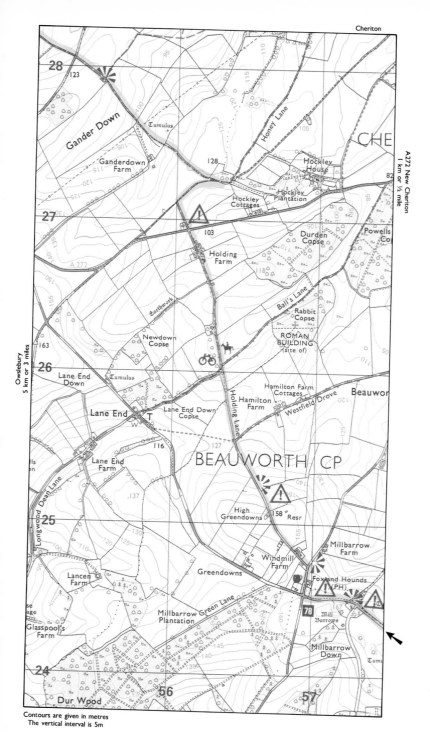

A272 New Cheriton
1 km or ½ mile

Owslebury
5 km or 3 miles

Gander Down

Tumulus

Ganderdown
Farm

Honey Lane

Hockley
House

CHE

Hockley
Plantation

Hockley
Cottages

Holding
Farm

Durden
Copse

Powells
Co

A 272

Earthwork

Ball's Lane

Rabbit
Copse

ROMAN
BUILDING
(site of)

Newdown
Copse

Lane End
Down

Tumulus

Hamilton Farm
Cottages

Beauwor

Lane End

T

Lane End Down
Copse

Hamilton
Farm

Westfield Drove

Holding Lane

BEAUWORTH CP

Lane End
Farm

High
Greendowns

158 Resr

Millbarrow
Farm

Longwood Dean Lane

Lancen
Farm

Windmill
Farm

Greendowns

Foxand Hounds
(PH)

Glasspool's
Farm

Millbarrow Green Lane
Millbarrow
Plantation

78

Mill
Barrows

Millbarrow
Down

Tum

Dur Wood

56

57

Contours are given in metres
The vertical interval is 5m

145

Continue north-west from Gander Down for 275 yards (250 metres) through a wooden bridle gate next to a field gate, across a road (Rodfield Lane), and keep heading north-west for about 1¼ miles (2 km) over undulating 'prairie' to Round Clump.

Just north of Round Clump, at a group of farm buildings and a cottage, you change direction and head south-west. Rising towards Cheesefoot Head, the landscape becomes arable again, with groups of trees around you and glimpses of Winchester to the west of Chilcomb Down. Beside Great Clump the Way passes between barbed-wire fences, with a line of beech trees and a mixed woodland to the east. Then it becomes a beautiful beech archway with fine views out to the scarp slope. To the west you can see the block of tree-planting on Telegraph Hill **79**.

The path passes just to the north of Cheesefoot Head car park to a bridle gate by the roadside. Cross the road very carefully here, and go through a metal field gate. The Way is not at all clear as you turn north-west in the middle of this narrow arable field, but head towards the southernmost corner of the rectangular coniferous woodland on Telegraph Hill. As you approach the trees, the views to the south and south-west begin to open up, and you can see as far as the oil refinery at Fawley. At the tumulus near Telegraph Hill, the views over Winchester

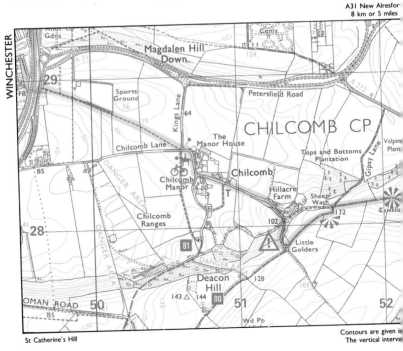

are particularly spectacular. From here, turn westwards, down towards Deacon Hill **80**. The Way is a farm track with a windbreak plantation on the south-west side. It can be muddy.

At a path junction, marked 'Sheep Wash' on the map, the Way kinks south then goes gently south-west again towards Deacon Hill **80**. At Little Golders the trail turns north-west down a sunken, metalled track, away from a flagpole and sign that warn of army ranges. Drop steeply north towards Hillacre Farm, past a fingerpost pointing east back up the hill as the road curves round into Chilcomb. As you enter Chilcomb, notice the old, black, tarred and tile-roofed granary sitting astride 'staddle stones', designed to keep out the rats. There is a large, brick barn at Sunshine Manor, which was once a group of three farmworkers' cottages. The road curves northwards at Chilcomb Manor and then on to The Manor House.

At the village pond, turn west to Kings Lane, and at the junction with Chilcomb Lane go over a stile and down a headland path, beside a rabbit-proof fence, in a north-westerly direction towards Winchester. From this junction you can divert due south to Chilcomb Church **81** up a headland path. This early Saxon church is worth a visit; it still uses a bell cast in 1380. The ranges are clearly visible against the hillside to the west.

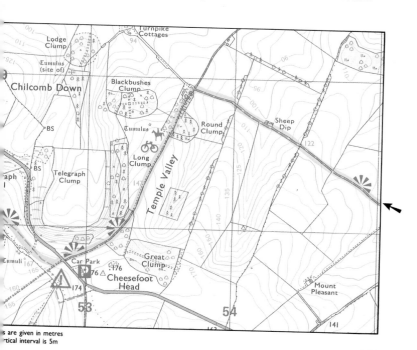

s are given in metres
rtical interval is 5m

Return to the junction at Kings Lane and head north-west along a footpath with Magdalen Hill Down, largely covered in scrub, to your north. Horseriders and cyclists currently have to end their route at Chilcomb until the footpath shown on the map is upgraded to bridleway status. To the south you can see the Iron Age hill fort of St Catherine's Hill. However, the ridges you see from this point on the walk are not the Iron Age defences but part of the city's sewage works.

Having travelled peacefully all this way from Eastbourne, it is a jolt to be passing over all the rushing traffic of the M3. At the far side of the bridge, turn north for 275 yards (250 metres), parallel to the motorway, and at a T-junction turn west towards The Soke in Winchester.

Pass All Saints Parish Church, a well-built, knapped flint Victorian building, and go to the junction of Canute Road and Highcliffe Road, where there is a general store. From here go gently down Petersfield Road and East Hill to the King's Arms and Blackboy's Pub. Turn north up Chesil Street towards the city centre. At the roundabout turn west into Winchester, the Saxon capital of England. The entrance to the youth hostel **82** at the City Mill is to be found down Water Lane, almost opposite Chesil Street.

You have now completed the South Downs Way. Well done!

WINCHESTER

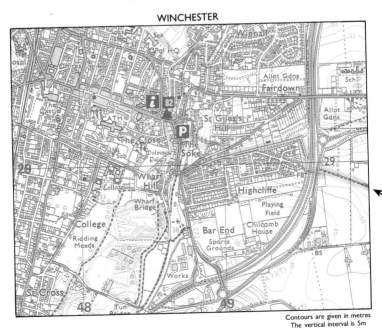

Contours are given in metres
The vertical interval is 5m

PART THREE

USEFUL
INFORMATION

Transport

Rail

There are regular services to major towns at the start and finish of the Way, and to other villages and towns either nearby or along the route.

You can gain access to the Way via the Eastbourne–Hastings trains from London (Victoria) every hour and alight at either Plumpton, Cooksbridge (basically commuter stations), Lewes, Glynde, Berwick, Polegate, or Eastbourne (change at Lewes for Newhaven and Seaford via Southease). Regular trains also go from London (Victoria) to Brighton via Hassocks, and there are more westerly services to Amberley and Arundel via Pulborough. There are also good services south of the Downs via Shoreham, Worthing and Chichester. Trains also go from Waterloo to Petersfield and Winchester. You may take bicycles on trains.

For passenger train information ring:

London (01) 928 5100
Brighton (0273) 206755
Horsham (0403) 62218
Portsmouth (0705) 825771
Southampton (0703) 229393

Buses

Since deregulation in October 1986, local and country bus services have been operated by a wide variety of companies. The sources change so rapidly that it is impossible to produce a serviceable public transport guide to the South Downs Way.

Check with the bus companies and authorities listed below to get an up-to-date picture.

East Sussex Highways and Transportation Department, Phoenix Causeway, Lewes, BN7 1UE. Tel. Lewes (0273) 482123. (They publish a bus map for visitors to the county.)

West Sussex Surveyors and Highways Department, Tower Street, Chichester, PO19 1RH. Tel. Chichester (0243) 777556. (They publish *Connections Winchester* and *Connections Petersfield*.)

Hampshire County Surveyors, The Castle, Winchester, SO22 8UJ. Tel. Winchester (0962) 68944.

Kent County Surveyors, Sandling Block, Springfield, Maidstone, ME14 2LQ. Tel. Maidstone (0622) 696996.

Bus companies operating services near or across the South Downs Way (1989). Timetables available from:

Southdown Motors Services Ltd (administrative office: Walwers Lane, Lewes, BN7 2JX), the major operator in the area. Enquiries from:

Eastbourne	Tel. Eastbourne (0323) 27354
Main enquiries Lewes	Tel. Lewes (0273) 474441
Bognor	Tel. Lewes (0273) 865204
Main enquiries Chichester	Tel. Lewes (0273) 779319
Littlehampton	Tel. Littlehampton (0903) 721148
Worthing	Tel. Littlehampton (0903) 37661
Main enquiries Hillsea	Tel. Hillsea (0705) 696911

Hastings & District Transport Ltd (to Eastbourne), Beaufort Road, Silver Hill, St Leonards on Sea, Hastings, E. Sussex, TN37 GP11. Tel. Hastings (0424) 433711.

Eastbourne Buses (Eastbourne to Beachy Head), Birch Road, Eastbourne, E. Sussex, BN23 6PD. Tel. Eastbourne (0323) 25106.

Southern Land Tours (occasional Eastbourne to Seaford), 139B Seaside, Eastbourne, E. Sussex, BN21 3PG. Tel. Eastbourne (0323) 35882.

Cuckmere Community Bus (Alfriston/Litlington to Seaford occasionally), N. Baker, Burlow Cottage, Milton Street, Nr Polegate, E. Sussex, BN25 1ST. Tel. Eastbourne (0323) 870014.

Autopoint Coaches (Polegate/Alciston/Firle village to Lewes), Gardner Street, Herstmonceaux, Nr Hailsham, E. Sussex, BN27 4LB. Tel. Eastbourne (0323) 832430.

Brighton & Hove Bus & Coach Co. Ltd. (Brighton to Devil's Dyke; also Pyecombe, Clayton, etc.), Conway Street, Hove, E. Sussex, BN3 3LT. Tel. Brighton (0273) 206666.

Brighton Buses (Patcham YHA to Brighton), Coombe Terrace, Lewes Road, Brighton, E. Sussex, BN2 4AX. Tel. Brighton (0273) 674881.

Maidstone & District Motor Services Ltd (Lewes, Brighton), Tunbridge Wells, Kent, TN4 9NX. Tel. Tunbridge Wells (0892) 26900/20221.

R.D.H. Services (Lewes, Brighton), 44 Dallas Lane, Barcombe, Near Lewes, E. Sussex, BN8 5DZ. Tel. Brighton (0273) 400711.

Lewes with its Norman priory and castle.

Cedar Travel (Midhurst, Petworth, Pulborough, Storrington to Worthing), 20 Teville Gate, Worthing, W. Sussex, BN11 1UA. Tel. Worthing (0903) 214321.

Sussex Bus (Petworth, Pulborough, Storrington and Chichester, Worthing and Horsham), Unit E2, Rudford Industrial Estate, Ford Airfield, Arundel, W. Sussex, BN18 0BS. Tel. Worthing (0903) 723372.

The Village Bus Committee for Amberley and Slindon. Sec. Mrs A.V. Beere, Pump Cottage, Church Hill, Slindon, Arundel, W. Sussex, BN18 0RB. Tel. Slindon (024 365) 446.

The Director of Education, W. Sussex County Council (Midhurst to Chichester via Graffham, Heyshott area), County Hall, Chichester, PO19 1RQ. Tel. Chichester (0243) 777786.

Tony's Coaches (Midhurst to Petersfield), 6 Slygates Cottages, Minstead, Midhurst, W. Sussex, GU29 0JL. Tel. Midhurst (073 081) 3324.

Westrings Coaches (Chichester to Midhurst), 48 Marine Drive West, West Wittering, Chichester, W. Sussex, PO20 8HH. Tel. Chichester (0243) 672411.

Sutton Bignor, Barlavington Country Bus Association (occasional service Petworth to Chichester), Mrs Stuart Dallyn, Keyzaston Farm, Sutton, Pulborough, W. Sussex, RH20 1PY. Tel. Pulborough (079 82) 257.

London & Country Bus (S & W) (occasional Horsham, Billingshurst to Chichester), Lesbourne Road, Reigate, Surrey, RH2 7LE. Tel. Reigate (073 72) 42411.

Harting Minibuses (occasional Harting to Petersfield and Chichester), Mr H.R. Lovell, Engine Farm, South Harting, Nr Petersfield, Hampshire, GU31 5QN. Tel. (073 085) 765.

Hants and Sussex Motor Services (Petersfield to Midhurst), Hollybank House, Emsworth, Hants, PO10 7ON. Tel. Emsworth (0243) 372045.

Portsmouth City Bus (Petersfield to Waterlooville and Portsmouth), Highland Road, Eastney, Portsmouth, PO4 9HE. Tel. Portsmouth (0705) 815903.

Alder Valley South (Guildford to Winchester, Hindhead to Petersfield, Hazlemere to Midhurst), 25 London Road, Hindhead, Surrey, GU26 6AB. Tel. Hindhead (042 873) 5757.

Hampshire Bus (Winchester to Petersfield), Bus Station, Winchester, Hants, SO23 9BA. Tel. Winchester (0962) 52352.

Southampton City Bus (Petersfield to Southampton via East Meon, etc), 226 Portswood Rd, Southampton, Hants, SO9 4XS. Tel. Southampton (0703) 701163.

Accommodation

All the local tourist information centres will help you to find accommodation (see list of addresses and telephone numbers below). Some libraries in West Sussex have certain tourist information but do not make accommodation bookings.

Eastbourne, E. Sussex: 3 Cornfield Terrace, Eastbourne, BN21 4NW. Tel. Eastbourne (0323) 411400.

Eastbourne, E. Sussex: Eastbourne Pier, Marine Parade, Eastbourne, BN21 3EL. Tel. Eastbourne (0323) 411800 (not open in winter months).

Seaford, E. Sussex: Station Approach, Seaford, BN25 2AR. Tel. Eastbourne (0323) 897426.

Lewes, E. Sussex: 32 High Street, Lewes, BN7 2LX. Tel. Lewes (0273) 471600.

Brighton, E. Sussex: Marlborough House, 54 Old Steine, Brighton, BN1 1EQ. Tel. Brighton (0273) 23755.

Hove, E. Sussex: King Alfred Leisure Centre, Kingsway, Hove, BN3 2WW. Tel. Brighton (0273) 720371.

Hove, E. Sussex: Town Hall, Norton Road, Hove, BN3 4AH. Tel. Brighton (0273) 775400.

Shoreham by Sea, W. Sussex: 86 High Street, Shoreham by Sea, BN4 5DB. Tel. Brighton (0273) 452086.

Worthing, W. Sussex: Town Hall, Chapel Road, Worthing, BN11 1HQ. Tel. Worthing (0903) 210022.

Worthing, W. Sussex: Marine Parade, Worthing, BN11 3PX. Tel. Worthing (0903) 210022.

Bognor Regis, W. Sussex: Belmont Street, Bognor Regis, PO21 1BJ. Tel. Bognor Regis (0243) 823140.

Chichester, W. Sussex: St Peter's Market, West Street, Chichester, PO19 1AH. Tel. Chichester (0243) 775888.

Petersfield, Hampshire: The Library, 27 The Square, Petersfield, Hampshire, GU32 3HH. Tel. Petersfield (0730) 68829.

Eastleigh, Hampshire: Town Hall Centre, Leigh Road, Eastleigh, Hampshire, SO5 4DE. Tel. Eastleigh (0703) 641261.

Winchester, Hampshire: The Guildhall, The Broadway, Winchester, Hampshire, SO23 9LJ. Tel. Winchester (0962) 67871.

East Sussex County Council produces two specialist lists of places to stay in the county: self-catering accommodation, budget-priced hotels and guest-houses; group accommodation centres. Write to East Sussex County Planning Department, Southover House, Southover Road, Lewes, E. Sussex, BN7 1YA. Tel. Lewes (0273) 481000.

Lewes District Council produces an accommodation guide for the area in and around Lewes, which covers quite a few places close to the Way. Write to Lewes District Council, Leisure Services Department, 32 High Street, Lewes, E. Sussex, BN7 2LX. Tel. Lewes (0273) 471600.

The South-East England Tourist Board produces a guide to accommodation along the South Downs Way in East and West Sussex (price 25p), but as yet has not included the extension through Hampshire. The guide largely covers rather expensive hotels. Write to The South-East England Tourist Board, The Old Brew House, Warwick Park, Tunbridge Wells, Kent, TN2 5TU. Tel. Tunbridge Wells (0892) 540766.

For information on youth hostels and membership of the YHA, contact The Regional Secretary, Youth Hostels Association, 25 Woodbridge Road, Guildford, Surrey, GU1 1DY. Tel. Guildford (0483) 300295.

There are youth hostels (often full – book in advance) at:

Beachy Head	Tel. Alfriston (0323) 21081.
Alfriston	Tel. Alfriston (0323) 870423.
Telscombe	Tel. Brighton (0273) 307077.
Patcham	Tel. Brighton (0273) 556196.
Truleigh Hill	Tel. Arundel (0903) 813419.
Arundel	Tel. Arundel (0903) 882204.
Winchester	Tel. Winchester (0962) 53723.

Camping

East Sussex Countryside Management Service, in conjunction with the Sussex Downs Project in West Sussex, produces a guide to camp sites and farmers sympathetic to campers along the Way. They are hoping to add bed and breakfast accommodation, low-cost hotels, youth hostels and bunkhouse barns to the list shortly. Price £1. Write to The Countryside Management Service, East Sussex County Council, c/o County Planning Department, Southover House, Southover Road, Lewes, E. Sussex, BN7 1YA. Tel. Lewes (0273) 477851/477893; or to Sussex Downs Conservation Project, c/o County Planning Dept, County Hall, Chichester, W. Sussex, PO19 1RL. Tel. Chichester (0243) 777618. At present there are no camp sites in the Hampshire section; but hopefully one might be provided in Queen Elizabeth Country Park.

Cyclists

Cyclists riding the Way have a fairly wide choice of shops that carry supplies and spares. Going east to west these are:

Heath Cycles, 106 Cavendish Place, Eastbourne, BN21 3TZ. Tel. Eastbourne (0323) 33404.

Phoenix Cycles, 217 Seaside, Eastbourne, BN22 7NR. Tel. Eastbourne (0323) 29060.

South Downs Cycles, 12 South Street, Eastbourne, BN21 4XF. Tel. Eastbourne (0323) 30795.

Cycleman, 46 Roseberry Avenue, Hampden Park, Eastbourne, BN22 9QV. Tel. Eastbourne (0323) 501157.

Tutt Bros, Cycle Shop, 26 Clinton Place, Seaford, BN25 1NP. Tel. Seaford (0323) 893130.

Sports and Cycles, 1 Meeching Road, Newhaven, BN9 9QX. Tel. Newhaven (0273) 513647.

Lewes Cycles, 28 Western Road, Lewes, BN7 1RP. Tel. Lewes (0273) 483399.

Rayment Cycles, 13/14 Circus Parade, New England Road, Brighton, BN1 4GW. Tel. Brighton (0273) 697617.

Bike UK, 126 Queens Road, Brighton, BN1 3WB. Tel. Brighton (0273) 821369.

J&J Cycles, 12 George St, Brighton, BN2 1RH. Tel. Brighton (0273) 618698.

Rigden Cycles, 3 Upper Gardner Street, Brighton, BN1 4AN. Tel. Brighton (0273) 681861.

Strudwick Cycles, 28 Oxford Street, Brighton, BN1 4LA. Tel. Brighton (0273) 609015.

M&J Cycles, 4 Beaconsfield Parade, Beaconsfield Road, Brighton, BN1 6DN. Tel. Brighton (0273) 555503.

Webbs, 92 Boundary Road, Hove, BN3 6GA. Tel. Brighton (0273) 417658.

Cooks For Cycles Ltd, 65 Portland Road, Hove, BN3 5DQ. Tel. Brighton (0273) 777775.

Rideaway Cycles, 101 High Street, Hurstpierpoint, BN6 9PU. Tel. Brighton (0273) 833246.

E.H. Gammans & Sons, Gordon Road, Shoreham by Sea, BN4 6WG. Tel. Brighton (0273) 452445.

Raleigh Cycle Centre, 38/40 Kingston Broadway, Shoreham by Sea, BN4 6TE. Tel. Brighton (0273) 596368.

The Worthing Cycle Shop, 2/3 Plaza Parade, Rowlands Road, Worthing, BN11 3JH. Tel. Brighton (0273) 208412.

Lancing Cycles, 20 Crabtree Lane, Lancing, BN15 9PQ. Tel. Lancing (0903) 752308.

John Spooner Cycles, 21 South Farm Road, Worthing, BN14 7AD. Tel. Worthing (0903) 32884.

John Wheeler Cycles, 3 Station Parade, Tarring Road, Worthing, BN11 4SS. Tel. Worthing (0903) 506272.

Mountain Bike Centre, 37/39, Eirene Road, Worthing, BN12 4DJ. Tel. Worthing (0903) 47171.

Mills Cycles, 98 George V Avenue, W. Worthing, BN11 5RP. Tel. Worthing (0903) 47307.

Chesil Cycle Depot, 73 North Walls, Winchester, SO23 8DA. Tel. Winchester (0962) 63703.

Horseriders

If you damage your gear, there are a limited number of saddlers along or near the Way. Going east to west these are:

Rider's Realm, 16 Crown Street, Eastbourne, BN21 1NX. Tel. Eastbourne (0323) 34496.

Polegate Saddlery, 3 Millfield, Station Road, Polegate, E. Sussex, BN26 6AS. Tel. Polegate (032 12) 3382.

Dragonfly Saddlery, Ditchling Crossroads, Ditchling, Sussex. Tel. Hassocks (07918) 4606.

Pyecombe Saddlery, London Road, Pyecombe, Nr Brighton, W. Sussex, BN4 7ED. Tel. Poynings (079 156) 213.

The Steyning Saddlery, 80 High Street, Steyning, BN4 3RD. Tel. Steyning (0903) 814268.

The Hove Tackroom, 424/426 Portland Road, Hove, Sussex, BN3 5SJ. Tel. Brighton (0273) 410200.

Petersfield Saddlery, Lyndum House, High Street, Petersfield, Hants, GU32 3JG. Tel. Petersfield (0730) 66816.

Farriers on or near the South Downs Way

East Sussex

Graham Baker, Glynde Forge, Glynde, Lewes, E. Sussex, BN8 6SU. Tel. Glynde (079 159) 474.

Frank and Roger Dean, The Forge House, Rodmell, Lewes, E. Sussex, BN7 3HS. Tel. Brighton (0273) 474740.

Roland Dubey, Wellingham Corner Cottage, Clayhill, Lewes, E. Sussex, BN8 5RX. Tel. Brighton (0273) 813154.

John Henty, Steel Works, Lower Road, Eastbourne, E. Sussex, BN21 1QE. Tel. Eastbourne (0323) 21938.

Glynde Church, where John Ellman, breeder of the Southdown sheep, is buried.

Mark Hobby, 22 Markstakes Corner, South Chailey, Lewes, E. Sussex, BN8 4BP. Tel. Brighton (0273) 400308.

David Kneller, 40 Stanfield Road, Lewes, E. Sussex, BN7 2SL. Tel. Brighton (0273) 476970.

Kenneth Larkin, The Kennels, 17 Priory Heights, Eastbourne, E. Sussex, BN20 8SR. Tel. Eastbourne (0323) 30301.

William Weeding, Forge Cottage, Ringmer, Lewes, E. Sussex, BN8 5NB. Tel. Brighton (0273) 813024.

West Sussex

Peter Fenton, Club Cottage, Top Road, Slindon, Arundel, W. Sussex, BN18 0RX. Tel. Chichester (0243) 772454.

David Froggatt, The Forge, West Dean, Chichester, W. Sussex, PO18 0RX. Tel. Chichester (0243) 63701.

Stephen Jefford, 6 Malthouse Close, Arundel, W. Sussex, BN18 9JF. Tel. Arundel (0903) 883676.

Robert Lockwood, Forge Cottage, Church Hill, Midhurst, W. Sussex, GU29 9NX. Tel. Midhurst (0730) 813208.

James Pimm, The Forge, Lower Beeding, Horsham, W. Sussex, RH13 6PS. Tel. Horsham (0403) 76686.

Michael Rollings, Rose Cottage, Lower Beeding, Horsham, W. Sussex, RH13 6PS. Tel. Horsham (0403) 76479.

Sidney Smith, 15 Mant Road, Petworth, W. Sussex, GU28 0EH. Tel. Petworth (0798) 42330.

Colin White, Great Todham Farm House, Ambersham, Midhurst, W. Sussex, GU29 0BU. Tel. Midhurst (0730) 816819.

Donald Wilkinson, The Forge, Funtington, Chichester, W. Sussex, PO18 9LL. Tel. Chichester (0243) 575577.

John Behan, 18 Guillods Cottages, Graffham, Petworth, W. Sussex, GU28 0NR. Tel. Petworth (0798) 6265.

Frederick Couch, 390 Stone Cottages, Easebourne Lane, Midhurst, W. Sussex, GU29 9BW. Tel. Midhurst (0730) 814438.

Henry Alston, 1 Greenfields, Sutton, Pulborough, W. Sussex, RH20 1PP. Tel. Petworth (0798) 7302.

Mark Broadbridge, Norwood Equestrian Centre, Norwood Lane, Graffham, Petworth, W. Sussex, GU28 0QG. Tel. Petworth (0798) 6338.

Jeremy Whaley, Elkham Farmhouse, Balls Cross, Petworth, W. Sussex, GU28 9JT. Tel. Horsham (0403) 77563.

Hampshire

Michael and Richard Moss, The Forge, 75 Froxfield Green, Petersfield, Hants, GU32 1DQ. Tel. Petersfield (0730) 63536.

Alan and David Povey, The Forge, Owslebury, Winchester, Hants, SO21 1LY. Tel. Winchester (0962) 74473.

Bernard Malone, 23 Shepherds Road, Winchester, Hants, SO23 8NR. Tel. Winchester (0962) 62662.

Vets

In case your horse is injured or your dog gets sick! This list is not comprehensive but it covers some of the ground (east to west). If these vets cannot help, try the Yellow Pages for more information.

Eastbourne: St Anne's Veterinary Group, 6 St Anne's Road, Eastbourne, BN21 2DJ. Tel. Eastbourne (0323) 640011 (24-hour emergency service; horses and dogs).

Lewes: Teakle, Rees & Partners, 21 Cliffe High Street, Lewes, BN7 2AH. Tel. Brighton (0273) 473232 (24-hour emergency service; horses and dogs).

Brighton: Philcox & Pepper, 57 Warren Way, Woodingdean, Brighton, BN2 6PH. Tel. Brighton (0273) 302609 (24-hour emergency service; horses and dogs).

Steyning: Crossway Veterinary Group, 2 High Street, Steyning, BN4 3GG. Tel. Steyning (0903) 816428 (24-hour emergency service tel. Storrington (090 66) 3040; horses and dogs).

Arundel: Ashton & Partners, The Tortington Equine Centre, Arundel, BN18 0BJ. Tel. Worthing (0903) 883050 (horses).

Storrington: Crossway Veterinary Group, The Surgery, 43A School Hill, Storrington, RH20 4NA. Tel. Storrington (090 66) 3040 (horses and dogs).

Pulborough: Arun Veterinary Group, 121 Lower Street, Pulborough, RH20 2BP. Tel. Pulborough (079 82) 2089/80 (24-hour emergency service tel. Midhurst (073 081) 3940; horses and dogs).

Chichester: Downland Veterinary Group, 2 Stirling Road, Chichester, PO19 2EN. Tel. Chichester (0243) 786101 (24-hour emergency service; horses and dogs).

Petersfield: Walmsley & Partners, Home Park, Forest Mere, Liphook, GU30 2JG. Tel. Liphook (0428) 723594 (24-hour emergency service; horses).

Winchester: Watson & Kennedy, Stable Close Veterinary Clinic, St Cross, Winchester, SO23 9TB. Tel. Winchester (0962) 841001 (24-hour emergency service; horses and dogs).

Local facilities (S=south of the Way)

Eastbourne: A large town with all facilities. Banks, youth hostel, places of interest, railway station, beach access.

Birling Gap: Pub, café, hotel, telephone, public toilets, car park, beach access.

East Dean: Pub, restaurant, store, post office, telephone, postbox, petrol station.

Seaford: A medium-sized town with all facilities, including tourist information, beach access, banks, railway station.

Westdean: Telephone, forestry information board, postbox.

Jevington: Pub, restaurant, tea rooms, car park, telephone, postbox.

Folkington: Postbox.

Wilmington: Pub, telephone, postbox, places of interest, car park, hotel, public toilets, restaurant, petrol station.

Litlington: Pub, tea gardens, telephone, postbox.

Milton Street: Pub, camping, telephone, postbox.

Alfriston: Pubs, cafés, restaurants, hotels, shops, post office, postbox, telephone, car parks, public toilets, youth hostel, place of interest.

Berwick: Pub, telephone, postbox.

Alciston: Pub, telephone, postbox.

Selmeston: Pub, postbox, telephone, petrol station, police house, restaurant.

West Firle: Firle Place open 2–5 p.m. June to September, including restaurant and teas, postbox, post office shop, telephone, pub.

Southease: Postbox, railway station.

Rodmell: Pub, forge and farrier, telephone, postbox, petrol station, car park, place of interest.

Iford: Telephone, postbox.

Kingston: Pub, telephone, postbox, shop.

Newmarket: Pub, petrol station, restaurant.

Lewes: Small historic town with most facilities. Banks and places of interest.

Offham: Pub, tea rooms, telephone, postbox.

Plumpton: Pub, telephone, postbox, petrol station, camping to north at Plumpton Green.

Westmeston: Telephone, postbox.

Ditchling: Car park, pubs, public toilets, petrol station, shops, post office, tea rooms, place of interest, saddlers, postbox, restaurants.

Clayton: Pub, postbox.

Pyecombe: Petrol station, pub, saddlers just to north of village.

Brighton: Large town with all facilities, including youth hostel, railway station, places of interest, etc.

Poynings: Pub, post office, shop, telephone.

Fulking: Pub, post office, shop.

Bramber: Pub, shops, restaurants, public toilets, hotel, place of interest.

Steyning: Large village with very good facilities, public toilets, car park, shops, banks, post office, hotels, library and tourist information, saddler.

Wiston: Post office, telephone, teas.

Washington: Pubs, petrol station, hotel, camping, post office, shop, telephone.

Storrington: Large village with good facilities, including pubs, restaurants, shops, banks, chemists, post office, telephone, petrol station, library with tourist information, car park, police house.

Arundel: Small historic town with most facilities and castle.

Amberley: Pubs, restaurant, café, telephone, postbox, railway station, places of interest, post office.

The old clock tower at Steyning, just off the Way.

Houghton: Pub, telephone, postbox.

Bury: Pub, telephone, post office, store, postbox.

West Burton: Postbox.

Bignor: Telephone, place of interest.

Sutton: Pub, postbox, jam and pickle shop.

Barlavington: Postbox.

Duncton: Pub, telephone, postbox.

Graffham: Pubs, post office, shop, postbox, petrol station.

Heyshott: Pub, telephone, postbox.

Cocking: Pubs, post office, telephone, postbox, shop, petrol station.

East Dean(S): Post office, store, petrol station, pub, postbox, telephone.

Charlton(S): Pub, postbox, telephone, hotel.

Singleton(S): Pubs, post office, shop, postbox, doctor, telephone, police house, teas, gallery.

West Dean(S): Pub, post office, shop, telephone, postbox, teas, car park, place of interest.

Midhurst: Small town with most facilities, including place of interest.

Bepton: Telephone, postbox, hotel.

Didling: Postbox.

Treyford: Postbox.

Elsted: Postbox, telephone, pub, post office (occasional).

East Harting: Telephone, postbox.

South Harting: Police house, postbox, pubs, telephone, public toilets, post office, shops.

Buriton: Post office, shop, telephone, pubs.

Chalton(S): Pub, telephone.

Petersfield: Small town with most facilities, railway station.

Clanfield(S): Pub, post office, shop.

East Meon: Post office, pub, shop.

West Meon: Pub, post office, shop, telephone.

Warnford: Pub.

Meonstoke, Corhampton, Exton: Pubs, post office, shop, telephone.

Kilmeston: Telephone.

Beauworth: Pub.

Cheriton: Pubs, post office, store, petrol station.

Chilcomb: Postbox, telephone.

Winchester: Historic city with all facilities, railway station, places of interest, cathedral.

Local organisations

If you have enjoyed your trip, you may wish to join, or make a financial contribution to, some of the organisations that help to conserve and manage the Downs:

Hampshire Field Club, Secretary, King Alfred College, Winchester, SO22 4NR. (Interested in all matters archaeological.)

Hampshire & Isle of Wight Naturalists Trust, 71 The Hundred, Romsey, Hants, SO51 8BZ. Tel. Romsey (0794) 513786. (Owns and manages land of wildlife interest.)

The National Trust, Estate Office (Kent & E. Sussex), Scotney Castle, Lamberhurst, Tunbridge Wells, Kent. Tel. Tunbridge Wells (0892) 890651, or (Southern Region), Polesden Lacey, Dorking, Surrey, RH5 6BD. Tel. Bookham (0372) 53401. Manages land and buildings of conservation significance.)

The Society of Sussex Downsmen, 93 Church Road, Hove, E. Sussex, BN3 2BA. Tel. Brighton (0273) 777906. (Lobbies against development on the Downs. Keeps an eye on all rights of way.)

South Downs Rangers, Tower House, North Street, Lewes, E. Sussex, BN7 2PE. Tel. Brighton (0273) 477851/477893. (Undertake practical voluntary work on all rights of way and conservation areas. Also advise and help visitors to the Downs.)

The Sussex Archaeological Society, Barbican House, 169 High Street, Lewes, BN7 1YE. Tel. Brighton (0273) 474379. (Encourages study of local history and archaeology, and conserves ancient buildings and monuments.)

The Sussex Wildlife Trust, Woods Mill, Henfield, W. Sussex, BN5 9SD. Tel. Brighton (0273) 492630 (Owns and manages land of wildlife interest.)

Other useful addresses

Association of Lightweight Campers, c/o Camping and Caravanning Club, 11 Lower Grosvenor Place, London, SW1W 0EY.

British Butterfly Conservation Society, Tudor House, Quorn, Loughborough, Leicestershire, LE1 28AD. Tel. Loughborough (0509) 412870. Local branch: Denis Day, 26 Manor House, Hassocks. Tel. Hassocks (079 18) 5754.

British Herpetological Society (reptiles), c/o Zoological Society, Regent's Park, London, NW1. Tel. London (01) 581 2657. (Local branch: 28 Old Fort Road, Shoreham by Sea, Sussex, BN4 5RJ.)

British Horse Society, British Equestrian Centre, Stoneleigh, Kenilworth, Warwickshire, CB8 2LR. Tel. Coventry (0203) 696697.

Conchological Society of Great Britain & Ireland (snails), Dr Martin J. Willing, (Conservation Officer), 14 Goodwood Close, Midhurst, W. Sussex, GU29 9JG. Tel. Midhurst (073 081) 4790.

Cyclists' Touring Club, Cotterall House, 69 Meadrow, Godalming, Surrey, GU7 3HS. Tel. Godalming (048 68) 7217.

Countryside Commission (headquarters), John Dower House, Crescent Place, Cheltenham, Glos, GL50 3RA. Tel. Cheltenham (0242) 521381.

Countryside Commission (South-East Regional Office), 71 Kingsway, London, WC2B 6ST. Tel. London (01) 831 3510.

Farriers Register Council, Mr B. Kavanagh, PO Box 49, East of England Showground, Peterborough, PE2 0GU. Tel. Peterborough (0733) 234451.

Mountain Bike Club of Great Britain, 3 The Shrubbery, Albert St, St Georges, Telford, TF2 9AS, or tel. London (01) 378 1944.

Nature Conservancy Council (South-East Regional Office), The Old Candlemakers, West Street, Lewes, E. Sussex, BN7 2NZ. Tel. Brighton (0273) 476595.

Ordnance Survey, Romsey Road, Maybush, Southampton, SO9 4DH. Tel. Southampton (0703) 792792.

Ramblers' Association, 1–5 Wandsworth Road, London, SW8 2XX. Tel. London (01) 582 6878. (Their annual yearbook has many bed and breakfast addresses; available free to members; available to non-members from major bookshops and newsagents for £2.95.)

Royal Society for the Protection of Birds, The Lodge, Sandy, Bedfordshire, SG19 2DL. Tel. Sandy (0767) 80551.

South-East England Regional Tourist Board (Kent, E. Sussex and Surrey), 1 Warwick Park, Tunbridge Wells, TN2 57A. Tel. Tunbridge Wells (0892) 540766.

Southern Tourist Board (Hampshire, East Dorset and Wiltshire), 40 Chamberlayne Road, Eastleigh, Hampshire, SO5 5JH. Tel. Eastleigh (0703) 620006.

Guided walks

In East and West Sussex the two county councils jointly produce an annual leaflet of guided walks, many of which are on the South Downs. Write to either: The Countryside Management Service, c/o County Planning Department, Southover House, Southover Road, Lewes, E. Sussex, BN7 1YA; or The County Secretary, West Sussex County Council, County Hall, Chichester.

Bibliography

Armstrong, Roy, *A History of Sussex* (Phillimore).

Beamish, Tufton, *Battle Royal* (Frederick Muller, 1965).

Brandon, Peter (ed.), *The South Saxons* (Phillimore).

——, *Sussex* (Making of the English Landscape Series) (Hodder & Stoughton, 1974).

Brent, Colin, *Historic Lewes and its Buildings* (Lewes Town Council).

—— and Rector, *Victorian Lewes* (Phillimore, 1980).

Comber, H. (ed.), *Along the South Downs Way to Winchester* (with accommodation list) (Eastbourne Rambling Club, 1985).

Darby, Ben, *South Downs* (Hale, 1976).

—— *View of Sussex* (Hale, 1975).

Delorme, Mary, *Curious Sussex* (Hale, 1987).

Green, E.G., *The South Downs Way* (Ramblers' Association, 1970).

Harrison, David, *Along the South Downs Way* (Cassell, 1958).

Jebb, Miles, *Guide to the South Downs Way* (Constable, 1984).

Meynell, Esther, *Small Talk in Sussex* (Hale, 1973).

Moore, Christopher, *Green Roof of Sussex* (Middleton Press, 1984).

Parker, Mary, *Riding and Road Safety Explained* (Southdown Promotions, 1987).

Perkins, Ben, *South Downs Walks for Motorists* (Frederick Warne, 1987).

Piper, A. Cecil, *Alfriston: The Story of a Sussex Downland Village* (Frederick Muller, 1974).

Pyatt, E.C., *Chalkways of South and South-East England* (David & Charles, 1974).

Smith & Haas, *Writers in Sussex* (Redcliffe, 1985).

Taylor, Rupert, *The East Sussex Village Book*, (Countryside Books, 1986).

Teuiot, Charles, *Walks along the South Downs Way* (Spurbooks, 1973).

Thornton, Nicholas, *Sussex Shipwrecks* (Countryside Books, 1988).

Webb, Montague, *Pictional Maps of the South Downs Way* (Napier Publications, 1975).

Westacott, H.D., *South Downs Way* (Penguin, 1983).

Wills, Barclay, *Bypaths in Downland* (Methuen, 1927).

Youth Hostels Association, *The South Downs Way* (1975).

Ordnance Survey Maps covering the South Downs Way

Landranger Maps (scale: 1:50 000): 185, 197, 198, 199

Pathfinder Maps (scale: 1:25 000): 1264 (SU42/52),
   1265 (SU62/72), 1285 (SU61/71), 1286 (SU81/91)
   1287 (TQ01/11), 1288 (TQ21/31), 1306 (TQ00/10)
   1307 (TQ20/30), 1308 (TQ40/50), 1324 (TV49/59/69)

Motoring Maps: Reach the South Downs Way by using Routemaster Map 9 (scale 1:250 000), 'South-East England'.

A note to the National Trail Guide user

We hope you like your National Trail Guide.

A great deal of care has been given to accuracy and clarity in compiling these guides but, inevitably, improvements can be made.

To help the publishers in making these books as accurate and useful as possible, your comments and criticisms are welcomed. Please write, giving your own name, address and postcode, and stating which guide(s) you have bought, to the following Freepost address (no stamp required): Countryside Commission, Freepost (GR 1422), Cheltenham, Glos, GL50 3BR.

In return we are offering a new service to you, the user. You will receive a newsletter containing additional information and revisions to help you make the most of the guides and enjoy your walks to the full.